FAIRBANKS

Alaska's Heart of Gold

A Traveler's Guide

Text by Tricia Brown
Photographs by Roy Corral

ALASKA NORTHWEST BOOKS™

For Perry, who I found in Fairbanks

ACHNOWLEDGMENTS—In conducting research for the historical segments of this book, I relied heavily on the excellent publications you'll find listed in "Recommended Reading." Certainly, not all researchers and interpreters of history are gifted storytellers. The best writers of Fairbanks history, in my opinion, include Bill Hunt, Claus-M. Naske, Lael Morgan, and the brothers Cole—Dermot and Terrence. Thank you all for your good work. My personalized perspectives of life in Fairbanks come from eight years of living in the Golden Heart City—eight hard winters without a garage, eight summers still perfect in my memory. Thank you to all the Stinsons, my Olsen girls, the Clarks, and friends as close to me as relatives, who helped make my Fairbanks years among my fondest.

—T.B.

I gratefully acknowledge the warm welcome I received in Fairbanks from Jim and Karin Gillis, Richard and Judi Gumm, and Ed and Jackie Debevec.

—R.C.

Library of Congress Cataloging-in-Publication Data

Brown, Tricia.
    Fairbanks, Alaska's heart of gold: a traveler's guide / text by Tricia Brown ; photographs by Roy Corral.
        p.   cm.
    Includes bibliographical references (p.92) and index.
    ISBN 0-88240-528-4 (alk. Paper)
    1. Fairbanks (Alaska)—Guidebooks. 2. Fairbanks Region (Alaska)—Guidebooks. I. Corral, Roy, 1946-   . II. Title

    F914.F16 B76 2000
    917.98'6—dc21   99-054835

PHOTOS—*Front cover:* View from the rear of *Discovery III; Pages 1-2, 95-96:* Winter's sunset emblazes clouds above spruce forest; *Page 3:* Athabascan boy; *Page 5:* A warm welcome. *Page 92:* A familiar street sign in Fairbanks.

President/Publisher: Charles M. Hopkins
Editorial Staff: Douglas A. Pfeiffer, Ellen Harkins Wheat, Timothy W. Frew, Tricia Brown, Jean Andrews, Alicia I. Paulson, Julia Warren
Production Staff: Richard L. Owsiany, Susan Dupere
Designer: Constance Bollen, cb graphics

Printed on acid- and elemental-chlorine-free recycled paper in the United States of America

Contents

Fairbanks, from Trading Post to City

As cities go, Fairbanks hasn't been around long. Antique collectors in Fairbanks have end tables, even cups and saucers, older than the historic cabins of the town. Fairbanks is more like a teenager in a growth spurt, like the knobby-kneed yearling moose that occasionally wander into town. Even so, this frontier community has matured rapidly in its first hundred years. And as it grew, Fairbanks acquired a nickname that reflected not only its beginnings, but its geographic location and its attitude toward strangers: Alaska's Golden Heart City.

From a log-cabin trading post on a remote river in the subarctic, Fairbanks has bloomed into an unpretentious metropolis that is Alaska's second-largest city, home to 32,000 people. It's the seat of government for the Fairbanks North Star Borough, this state's version of a county, in which another 52,000 people live among a sprinkling of smaller towns and two military installations.

A century ago, this place was a broad valley forested with birch, spruce, and aspen. Wildlife was plentiful, and the area's indigenous people, the Athabascan Indians, hunted big game, fished the rivers and lakes, and trapped small furbearers such as foxes, rabbits, beavers, and muskrats. Geese and ducks provided

"Unknown First Family" stands in Golden Heart Park.

both meat and eggs. With a few exceptions, the Interior Natives lived peaceably with the Westerners who started showing up in the late 1800s to explore, trade goods, or look for gold. But when news of a gold strike near Pedro Dome leaked in 1902, a stampede resulted, and a frontier town sprang up.

A century after its founding in 1901, Fairbanks is a place name that's recognized across the country. It evokes the spirit of an independent people and testifies to endurance in a harsh environment. In every sense, it's synonymous with the word *gold*.

There really was gold in them-thar hills, and in late July 1902, an Italian immigrant named Felix Pedro made a major strike nearby. For many years, the anniversary of Pedro's discovery has been celebrated in the biggest party of the summer: "Golden Days," a mid-July week of sidewalk sales, gold-panning demonstrations, sourdough pancake breakfasts, and pioneer socials culminating in a community-boosting parade with the word "gold" somewhere in the theme.

Today Fairbanks is both a destination and hub for tourism, international air cargo, and trucking, even though few roads thread beyond the residential areas and over the foothills. The forested valley and surrounding uplands still teem with wildlife, inviting residents outdoors in every season. The University of Alaska Fairbanks is renowned for leading work in aurora research and arctic biology, and its museum is a major tourist attraction. And, although Fairbanks is not the state's capital, it serves as an informal regional capital for the people of the Interior. What's more, Fairbanks has developed into the end goal for adventurers everywhere who want to see for themselves what it takes to live at the northern edge of the country. About 325,000 visitors come through each summer; new pioneers arrive every week.

Living in Fairbanks year-round, its people become attuned to its natural cycles of light and dark, heat and cold, hunting seasons and fishing seasons, time to put in the garden and time to can the beets. And yet, no matter how long they live here, the dramatic change of seasons comes as a shock: 21 hours of daylight in late June and, by late December, 21 hours of darkness; summer heat that burns the skin and causes cabbages to grow as big as beach balls and

Winter noonday sun rises above the Chena River.

winter's minus 40°F cold that freezes eyelashes together, shocks the lungs, and turns cars into thousand-pound paperweights.

Residents coexist with a wilderness that accepts and rejects their presence, sometimes within the same hour. A cow moose and calf are a welcome sight outside the window when you're reading a book on the couch. But when you head to your car, you'd better not be in the zone between mama and baby, or you're fair game. The false security of riding in a warm vehicle on a minus 20°F day can quickly shatter when the alternator belt breaks. The intoxication of the midnight sun lulls you into believing that another year here would be just fine; then suddenly it's early December, still dark at 10 A.M., and it feels as if gravity has tripled its power.

At last, a few days past winter solstice, right around Christmas Eve, the town is gaining daylight, first a few seconds a day, then eventually up to 7 minutes and more. The daily updates are broadcast during the TV weather reports and in the *Fairbanks Daily News-Miner*. The mantra becomes *We're gaining daylight, we're gaining daylight.* Then a jogger, his beard crusted over with frost, trots through a parking lot in the dim winter light, and you are amazed at what people can and will do because they love it here.

Through the cycles of extremes—the fluctuations of light and dark, of heat and piercing cold, of the economic ups and downs, and of personal biorhythms—Fairbanks remains a magnet for those who are able to discard their understanding of "normal" and see the wonder for what it is.

It was gold that built this place, and gold remains one of the reasons why people stay. But that gold comes in different forms. There's the heavy yellow metal that drives men to stampede. In folklore, there's gold in the hearts of the sweet but sinful ladies of the evening. Come autumn, there's the crisp, brilliant gold of the aspen and birch across the Tanana Valley. But perhaps the greatest treasure lies in the deep vein of gold—in the form of friendship, charity, and hospitality—drawn upon by locals who lean on one another in need and join again to celebrate in good times. In the golden warmth of Fairbanks, strangers quickly become friends. ■

FAIRBANKS AT A GLANCE

- **Population:** 31,601—Alaska's second-largest city.
- **Location:** Interior Alaska, 64° 50' N, 147° 43' W.
- **Area:** 31 square miles of land; 1 square mile of water.
- **Government:** Home-rule city within Fairbanks North Star Borough, population 83,928; borough communities also include College, Ester, Fox, Harding Lake, Moose Creek, North Pole, Pleasant Valley, Salcha, and Two Rivers.
- **Major waterways:** Chena and Tanana Rivers.
- **Average temperatures:** Winter, minus 12°F; summer, 60°F.
- **Extreme temperatures:** Recorded as low as minus 78°F in midwinter; as high as 93°F in summer.
- **Average annual precipitation:** 11.3 inches.
- **Hours of daylight:** 21 hours, May 10–August 2; less than 4 hours, November 18–January 24.
- **Indigenous people:** Athabascan Indians.
- **Settled:** 1901 by trader Captain E. T. Barnette.
- **Gold discovered:** 1902 by Felix Pedro in nearby Pedro Creek.
- **Named for:** Indiana Senator Charles Fairbanks in 1902. (Fairbanks became vice president under Theodore Roosevelt in 1904.)
- **Nearby military installations:** Fort Wainwright (formerly Ladd Field); Eielson Air Force Base.
- **Higher education:** University of Alaska Fairbanks, opened in 1922 as the Alaska Agricultural College and School of Mines with 6 students in attendance; now nearly 10,000 are enrolled.
- **Transportation:** Centrally located on major transportation corridor via Steese, Richardson, Elliott, Parks, Dalton, and Alaska Highways; small-aircraft hub for flights to bush communities; international and domestic jet traffic served by Fairbanks International Airport; public floatplane base on Chena River; terminus of state-owned Alaska Railroad.
- **Tourism:** 325,000 visitors each summer.

FAIRBANKS

Musk Ox Farm
(Large Animal
Research Station)

FARMERS LOOP ROAD

Fairbanks
Golf and
Country Cl

Mount McKinley
Viewpoint

University of
Alaska Fairbanks

UNIVERSITY AVENUE

COLL

PARKS HIGHWAY

③

TO ESTER:
Ester Gold Camp
Malemute Saloon
TO ANCHORAGE

GEIST ROAD

Deadman Slough

CHENA RIDGE ROAD

ALASKA

FAIRBANKS

CHENA PUMP ROAD

Chena
Pump House

⑲

③

㉚

Chena River

⑳

AIRPORT WAY

N

Chena
Marina
Airport

Fairbanks International Airport

UNIVERSITY AVENUE SOUTH

0 0.2 0.4 0.6 0.8 1.0
MILES

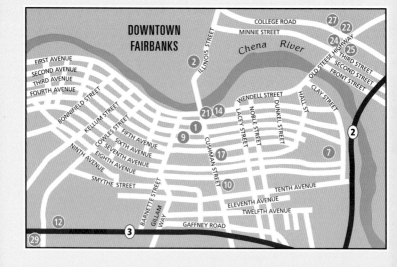

**DOWNTOWN
FAIRBANKS**

COLLEGE ROAD

MINNIE STREET

Chena River

ILLINOIS STREET

㉗ ㉒

㉔

OLD STEESE HIGHWAY

THIRD STREET

②

SECOND STREET

㉕

FIRST AVENUE

SECOND AVENUE

THIRD AVENUE

FOURTH AVENUE

BONNIFIELD STREET

KELLUM STREET

COWLES STREET

FIFTH AVENUE

SIXTH AVENUE

SEVENTH AVENUE

EIGHTH AVENUE

NINTH AVENUE

SMYTHE STREET

WENDELL STREET

LACEY STREET

NOBLE STREET

DUNKEL STREET

HALL ST.

CLAY STREET

FRONT STREET

㉑ ⑭

①

⑨

CUSHMAN STREET

⑰

②

⑦

⑩

TENTH AVENUE

ELEVENTH AVENUE

TWELFTH AVENUE

BARNETTE STREET

GILLAM WAY

GAFFNEY ROAD

⑫

AIRPORT WAY

③

㉙

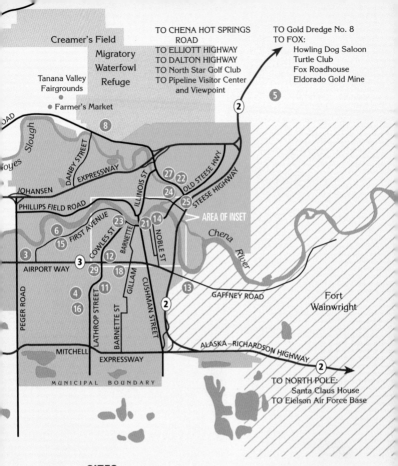

SITES

1. Alaska Public Lands Information Center
2. Alaska Railroad Depot
3. Alaskaland
4. Big Dipper Sports Center
5. Birch Hill Recreation Area
6. Carlson Center
7. Clay Street Cemetery Historical Site
8. Creamer's Field Migratory Waterfowl Refuge Visitor's Center
9. Downtown Post Office
10. Fairbanks Convention and Visitors Bureau
11. Fairbanks Memorial Hospital
12. Fairbanks North Star Borough Public Library
13. Fort Wainwright Main Gate and Visitor's Center
14. Golden Heart Plaza
15. Growden Park
16. Hez Rey Recreation Center
17. MACS Transit Center (Bus Depot)
18. Mary Siah Recreation Center
19. Pike's Landing
20. Riverboat *Discovery*
21. Visitor Information Log Cabin

SHOPPING

22. Bentley Mall
23. Downtown District
24. Fred Meyer
25. Gavora Mall
26. K-Mart
27. Sam's Club
28. Sears
29. Shopper's Forum
30. University Center

KODIAK 508
KOTZEBUE 441
NENANA 53
NOME 492
PRUDHOE BAY 489

ANCHORAGE 358
ARCTIC CIRCLE 194
BARROW 500
DELTA JCT. 98
DENALI PARK 120

CITY OF FAIRBANKS
ALASKA

Welcome to

FAIRBANKS

THE
GOLDEN
HEART
CITY

MILE 1523

"The OFFICIAL End of
the ALASKA HIGHWAY"

AMSTERDAM	6420
ATHENS	7728
BOMBAY	9289
CAIRO	5889
CALGARY	2038
CAPETOWN	10212
CHICAGO	3503
COPENHAGEN	6402
DALLAS	3852
DAWSON CITY	400
DAWSON CREEK	1521
DENVER	3152
EDMONTON	1887
GLASGOW	3892
GREAT FALLS	2375
GUADALAJARA	3847
GUAM	4717
HAMBURG	6464
HO CHI MINH CITY	5992
HONG KONG	8025
HONOLULU	3037
HOUSTON	4682
SYDNEY	7541
INUVIK	880
ISTANBUL	7625
JERUSALEM	5768
LISBON	7299

The
Golden Heart City

To many Americans, Fairbanks seems an exotic, even foreign destination. Perhaps this is remnant thinking from the days when U.S. soldiers stationed in Alaska received overseas pay. Every resident seems to have a story about a well-meaning person calling to ask if Alaska uses U.S. currency or if one needs a passport to cross the border. If only those callers could see the daily crowds at the golden arches, the kids in baggy jeans hanging out at the mall, the espresso junkies hotfooting it to work, or the people waiting in line for Steven Spielberg's latest release.

Despite Fairbanks' normal appearance, the folks in the Lower 48 have it right. This place is truly different. And so are the people who choose to live here.

First of all, Alaska itself is far, far away. Most map makers have grossly misled the public by putting a "Honey, I Shrunk the State" version of Alaska in a box off the coast of Baja. In land mass alone, Alaska's length and breadth is equal to one-fifth of all the Lower 48 states combined. Fairbanks is centrally located within the state and protected by two mountain ranges—the Brooks and Alaska Ranges—kind of like an island within an island. Just getting to Anchorage takes 45 minutes by jet. It's another 3 hours to fly to Seattle, the closest major city in the Lower 48.

The milepost marking the "end of the road."

This city is so geographically insulated that it's easy to overlook certain facts: in other towns, most people don't measure their worth by the number of years they've lived there. Most people don't line their windows with aluminum foil to keep the sun out at night. Elsewhere, they don't have a political party that calls for a reconsideration of the statehood vote. And in other places, drivers don't pull off the road to gape at the night sky while ribbons of color dance overhead—and then, mesmerized, stand in below-zero temperatures until they're almost hypothermic.

Fairbanks even has different vocabulary. "Headed Outside?" is asking if someone is leaving the state. A "sourdough" is an old-timer, and a new arrival is a "cheechako." A "wanigan" is a lean-to joined to a home. And few houses lack an "arctic entrance," which is made up of two sets of front doors with a small room between them so that freezing air doesn't come roaring into the house when the outside door is opened. It's also the place to strip off coats and boots and come inside in your stocking feet. For in Fairbanks, as elsewhere in Alaska, it is customary to leave your shoes at the door.

Unlike other small towns across the country, where people have known one another from birth, most of the people in Fairbanks are transplants. Consequently, Alaska-born adults are uncommon except among the region's Native Alaskans, the Athabascan Indians, whose family trees reach back thousands of years in the Interior. (The capitalization of the letter N matters. It's "Native Alaskan" with a capital N when you refer to an Indian or Eskimo, and "native" with a small n when you refer to any person born and raised in Alaska. That accounts for the puzzled look on a white guy's face when a tourist asks him if he's a native Alaskan. His answer is no, and no.)

Fairbanks is a town with cyclical prosperity, having grown in spurts since its first boom, the Tanana Valley gold rush of 1902. Other peaks occurred with the construction of two military bases and the Alaska Highway in the 1940s, and the trans-Alaska oil pipeline in the 1970s. Rebuilding after floods and fires injected money into the economy, too. And a deluge of oil royalty into state coffers ignited a building boom of libraries, convention centers, and

RUNNING WITH THE DOGS

DOG MUSHING IS ALASKA'S OFFICIAL STATE SPORT. But how did the term "mush" come to be associated with running dogs anyway? It's taken from the French word *mouche,* "to fly." And fly they do. One visit to the Jeff Studdert Mushing Hall off Farmers Loop Road will offer insight into the hobby and competitive sport that has developed around the northern peoples' love for dogs. Walk through the mini-museum or step outside to watch the recreational mushers and sprint races.

For a time, Fairbanks was the sled-dog racing capital, thanks to famed musher Leonhard Seppala, who won Nome's All-Alaska Sweepstakes in 1915, 1916, and 1917. With his lead dog, Togo, Seppala helped transport diphtheria serum to Nome in 1925, a trek reported in newspapers nationwide. He made Fairbanks his home for 19 years, adding excitement to the Winter Carnival sprint races.

In 1946, dog mushers organized a sled dog "derby," the grand-daddy to today's Open Class North American Championship, a sprint race covering 70 miles over 3 days during which the mushers' best times are combined.

Each February, Fairbanks hosts a long-distance sled-dog race connecting Fairbanks with Whitehorse, Yukon. The Yukon Quest International Sled Dog Race covers a thousand miles, over summits, along the Yukon River, across an international boundary, and through one-cabin "towns." Mushers rest in Carmacks, Dawson City, Eagle, and Circle City—towns made famous during the gold rush. From its first starting line on Second Avenue in 1984, the Quest has started or finished in Fairbanks, alternating each year, and continues a mushing tradition that remains an important part of local history. ■

other capital projects in the 1980s. During economic lulls, the city has learned to pinch back, wait it out, and pray for another boom. In the last 20 years, a growing Alaska tourism industry and rising oil prices have had favorable effects on Fairbanks' economy. Also,

ATHABASCAN FIDDLING FESTIVAL

LISTEN WITH YOUR EYES CLOSED and you could swear you were deep in the Ozarks, not tapping your toes in a Fairbanks dance hall. It's the annual Athabascan Old-Time Fiddling Festival, a 3-day event in which Native Alaskans provide the entertainment.

This is "fiddle" music, not violin performance. It's wild and fast or soft and mournful. But best of all, it's improbable: music of another century and another part of America swells through the hall as couples swing, jig, reel, and heel-and-toe. Although the Athabascan performers take great pride in the ancient songs and dances of their own culture, they also hold dear the old-time tunes that they grew up with. Their ancestors adopted the music from the trappers, prospectors, and traders who traveled along the Yukon River a century ago.

Athabascan fiddler Bill Stevens (above) led the way to organize the first festivals in the mid-1980s and continues to provide stellar entertainment with his own bright blue, electric fiddle. Talented musicians from all along the Yukon also highlight the program. The festival takes place in early November and is sponsored by the Institute of Alaska Native Arts, which celebrates and helps preserve Athabascan Indian traditions—even those that are just a century old. ■

Miss Ricki, an icon of Golden Days.

gold mining on a commercial level experienced a rebirth in the mid-1990s with the opening of Fort Knox, a gold mine just north of Fox, and other gold-mining enterprises.

Through the years, the annual mid-July celebration known as "Golden Days" has become an expression of pride among the people who have chosen to live in a town above the 65th parallel. The festival is such a popular event that it virtually overshadows the Independence Day observance earlier in the month. Every year, thousands of people choke the narrow streets of downtown Fairbanks, watching for their kids' Boy Scout troops, baton twirlers, or favorite float entries, such as the log cabin on wheels that's the Golden Days Jail. "Enforcers" dressed in Keystone Kops–style uniforms work the crowds looking for protective Golden Days pins, snatching folks off the sidewalks and tossing them inside. A spin of the jail's roulette wheel determines how much it'll cost to get out. Vamping on the jail's back porch is the buxom "Madame" Ricki in a sequined gown that's cut so low that it makes Mae West look like the girl next door.

At the head of the parade walks the winner of the annual Felix Pedro Look-alike Contest leading a mule with saddlebags full of

text continues on page 22

CREATIVE PLAYTIME

WHEN POET ROBERT SERVICE wrote of the "strange things done 'neath the Midnight Sun," he might well have meant certain sporting events in Fairbanks. Here's a taste of how Fairbanks plays.

Midnight Sun Baseball Game

For decades, a solstice night favorite has been the semi-pro baseball game that begins at 10:30 P.M. on June 21 or 22, and here's the hitch: they play with no artificial lights. The Alaska Goldpanners baseball team hosts the event, attracting hundreds who want to say they've seen it with their own eyes.

World Eskimo-Indian Olympics

Native people compete and celebrate their cultures in this annual sports event that includes traditional dances and a Miss WEIO competition. Among the games is the Ear Pull, in which contestants face each other, with a loop of string connecting one ear on each person. They lean back and grimace. Who will give up first? There's the Knuckle Hop, a Marines-style push-up on fists, only the men push off and move forward, inching along on a hardwood floor. The Blanket Toss, the One-Foot Kick, the Three-Man

Carry. You've not likely seen these before. The competition is fierce and exciting and takes place in late July, at the tail end of Golden Days.

Equinox Marathon

Judged the second-most-difficult marathon in the country, the race officially ushers in autumn each September. The grueling course begins on the University of Alaska campus and then wends through brilliant fall foliage on trails leading above treeline to the top of 2,364-foot Ester Dome and back again. The view is magnificent, as is the effort of the runners who come from around the country each fall to experience the Equinox.

Yukon 800

A wild, 2-day endurance race in riverboats follows 800 miles of the unforgiving Chena, Tanana, and Yukon Rivers. Three-person teams compete in customized 24-foot boats with 50-horsepower motors on a course from Fairbanks to Galena and back. Captain and crew are outfitted in wetsuits, helmets, life jackets, and usually kidney belts to support their organs as the boats bang along the rivers. One crew member steers and the other two are simply ballast with hands. A restaurant-bar named Pike's Landing, just off Airport Way, hosts the start- and finish-line festivities over the solstice holiday in late June.

Chatanika Days Outhouse Races

At Mile 28 Steese Highway lies a remnant gold camp, Chatanika, that each March hosts the Chatanika Days winter carnival with snowshoe races, bachelor auction, plenty of food, and free-flowing beer. But the highlight of the weekend is the outhouse races. Creatively titled, the custom-made "facilities" are built on skis, inner tubes, anything that promotes speed. Competitors trot alongside with one person inside. The starting line is at the Old Fairbanks Exploration Camp, and the finish is a mile away at Chatanika Lodge. ■

A competitor in the One-Foot Kick.

*Fairbanks boomed with the construction of the
trans-Alaska pipeline in the mid-1970s.*

"gold." A handlebar mustache and dark hair are the ticket for winning the contest, a nod to the Italian man who put this place on the map. Dressed in jeans, flannel shirt, and suspenders, old Felix doesn't actually look too different from many of the spectators— some of whom are modern-day gold miners.

Later in the day, the Big Dipper Sports Center is packed with spectators and competitors involved in the World Eskimo–Indian Olympics (WEIO). The unique games are as ancient as the Greeks', and the competition is equally stiff. The extended family of Interior Alaska Natives hosts potlucks, dances, a parka-making contest, and a scholarship contest for Miss WEIO.

A fun-filled social calendar propels the town through winter and draws the toughest of the tourists who come to shake hands with Fairbanks at its coldest. In February the thousand-mile Yukon Quest International Sled Dog Race begins or ends in Fairbanks, and in March the dog-mushing sprint races are at full speed. March also is a favorite month for fans of the World Ice Art Championships, an international ice-sculpting competition that's the centerpiece of the Fairbanks Winter Carnival. The carnival features entertainment, a cook-off, and creative snow games, such as snowshoe softball, to celebrate winter.

Just 2 miles from the Fairbanks city center, the northernmost university in the country is a cornerstone of the community. The University of Alaska Fairbanks is an important source of cultural fare, featuring the U of A Museum, Fairbanks Symphony Orchestra performances, nationally touring plays, student and faculty recitals, and readings and craft talks by visiting authors. It's also the site of the annual Summer Arts Festival, in which noted musicians from around the country arrive to lead workshops and perform in a week of public concerts. In addition, Fairbanks takes pride in the hot competition between UAF's Nanooks (a rough spelling of the Inupiat Eskimo word for "polar bear") and other teams from around the nation that compete in hockey, men's and women's basketball, and other athletic events. Each November, the university hosts Division I basketball teams from top American universities in the Top of the World Classic. And each September, the Equinox Marathon, a grueling race that attracts runners from around the country, begins and ends on campus.

Around Fairbanks, folks know how to avoid "cabin fever," that stir-crazy feeling that strikes when you spend too many days trapped indoors. The truth is, activity in Fairbanks slows only slightly during winter. Cabin fever, they might say, is the ailment of the solitary and the bored. For visitors and locals alike, each season in the Golden Heart City is cause to mark the calendar for the next event, enjoy it to its fullest, and look forward to still another. ■

The Land, the Elements, the People

It was 1:30 A.M. on a day in early June of 1885 when Army explorer Lieutenant Henry T. Allen rested on a ridge in the Alaska Range and gazed down upon the valley below. Allen wrote in his journal:

> From this, the most grateful sight it has ever been my fortune to witness was presented. We had nearly reached the "land of the midnight sun," to find in our front the "promised land." The sun was rising, but not in the east, in fact just two points east of north. . . . The views in advance and in rear were both grand; the former showing the extensive Tanana Valley with numerous lakes, and the low, unbroken range of mountains between the Tanana and Yukon Rivers. On this pass, with both white and yellow buttercups around me and snow within a few feet, I sat proud of the grand sight which no visitor save an [Athabascan Indian] had ever seen.

Leading a 3-man military expedition to obtain and evaluate information that would be "valuable and important, especially to

text continues on page 28

Snowshoe hare tracks dot spring snow in aspen forest.

■

WONDER IN THE HEAVENS

Midnight Sun

On June 21 or 22, the longest day of the year, Fairbanks will see 21 hours of daylight, framed on each side by twilight as the sun slips behind the edge of the surrounding mountains. For the full solstice experience, groups of photographers or just gawkers travel northeast for 108 miles to Eagle Summit on the Steese Highway, where, from an elevation of 3,624 feet, the midnight sun is visible above the horizon throughout the entire night. Time exposures every half hour yield incredible photos in which the midnight sun appears to be an orange-yellow ball skimming along the horizon.

Sundogs

On sharp, cold winter days, suspended ice crystals in the air sometimes form tiny prisms that reflect the sun's light. The result is the creation of a pair of wide, rainbow-like parentheses cupping each side of winter's low-lying sun.

Ice Fog

In the city, traffic slows to a crawl when the temperature drops well below zero and moisture hangs in the air in the form of ice crystals. The reflective specks reduce visibility to almost zero, and drivers have trouble seeing beyond the edge of their hoods. The cars' high beams make matters worse, as they do in normal fog. Because Fairbanks lies in a valley, the extremely cold air layers tend to linger in the valley bottom, with warmer and clearer air found in the surrounding hills. From the hills looking down, Fairbanks is nearly invisible under a gray blanket. Besides the deep cold, contributing factors include moisture from car exhaust and a general lack of wind in the Tanana Valley.

Aurora Borealis

Popularly called the northern lights, this natural light show has inspired myths and legends for thousands of years and continues to thrill viewers who endure deep cold to stand outside and watch the "performances." But what are the northern lights? Dr. Neil Davis, a professor of geophysics at the University of Alaska Fairbanks, offers this simplified explanation: "Fast incoming particles, electrons or protons, strike oxygen and nitrogen gases in the high atmosphere, causing them to

emit auroral photons." And yet a scientific understanding of the aurora is unnecessary for enjoyment. The color bars, curtains, and ribbons, pulsing and dashing across the heavens, never fail to entertain on cold, clear nights.

The northern lights are present year-round, but simply not visible when the sun lightens the sky. And in the southern hemisphere, a mirror image of the aurora borealis—called the aurora australis—is visible in the upper atmosphere above the South Pole.

Mirages

Atmospheric conditions in spring and fall can deliver a surprise. At certain times, people in Fairbanks will see Mount McKinley in the wrong direction on the horizon, oversized and dressed in a stunning shade of pink. It's actually a mirage, a mere reflection of the mountain's image cast against a screen of reflective particles in the air. ■

the military branch of the Government," Allen and his men would cover 1,500 miles and map the Copper, Tanana, and Koyukuk Rivers in less than 20 weeks' time. Allen's 1885 expedition also is credited with mapping the Suslota Pass, a gateway to the Tanana and Yukon Valleys.

On a clear day, from a mountain ridge or an airplane window, the Tanana Valley remains a breathtaking view to behold. The jagged Alaska Range and Mount McKinley lie to the south, and the Brooks Range to the north, like two sentinels refusing entry. The broad basin between them is forested with birch, spruce, and aspen. Shimmering lakes reflect the summer sky, and below, the braided Tanana River, cloudy with sediment, rolls toward the Yukon. From above, you can see oxbow lakes, segments of the Tanana that were cut off during natural changes in its course. In time, with no fresh water to feed them, the oxbows fill with sediment, the water disappears, and treeless scars are left behind. After many years, the blemishes fill with brush and trees.

Bounded on the north and south by these mountain ranges, the Tanana Valley is so well protected by natural walls that its weather patterns are unlike any other in the state. Even though it's nearly 400 miles closer to the Arctic Circle than Anchorage, this place is routinely 10° to 15° warmer in summer. Far from the chill and drizzle of Juneau and Anchorage's coastal climate, the Interior can boast of the best summers in the state. In fact, Fort Yukon once reached a record 100°F. And while the average summer temperature is 60°, most residents will swear that it's above 80° for most of that brief season. Lightning strikes are the most common cause of wildfires, tornadoes are nonexistent, and hot summer days often finish with a light, cooling shower.

Unfortunately for year-round residents, in winter those protective walls of the mountain ranges, so welcome in summer, act as sides of a bowl in which warm air rises. The coldest of the cold air lingers over the valley, trapped and still, because the mountains block the wind. On those days, a temperature inversion occurs, benefiting those who live in the warmer surrounding hills. Temperatures between the top and bottom of the hills can vary as much as 20°.

The Tanana River courses through a broad valley bordered by the Alaska Range to the south and forested hills to the north.

Many of the buildings and roads around Fairbanks were constructed on soil that's considered a civil engineer's nightmare. The problem is permafrost, and it accounts for why some roads buck and heave, why old-time cabins used to sink slowly into the ground, and why even new houses can break up and tip over in a few short years. (New building methods have been developed to prevent that from happening, however.)

Beyond Fairbanks, all of Interior Alaska, in fact, is geologically categorized as "discontinuous permafrost," meaning that beneath the ground cover, the soil is riddled with ice in places. In some instances, ice lenses have formed. With permafrost, ice particles fill in the spaces around the fine sediment, but with an ice lens, frozen water accumulates in a large pocket that, if it melts, creates a sinkhole on the surface.

*Many Athabascans still rely on trapping
as a source of income.*

The thawing and settling are accelerated when humans build heavy, heat-producing structures atop the icy soil. Pressure creates heat, and in these parts, heat melts the ground. To combat the problem, road builders have experimented with using Styrofoam layers and other ground blankets between the soil and road surface, and even white, heat-reflective paint on top, but most often, they just throw another layer of blacktop over the potholes or tear up the roller-coaster portions of road and start again. In home construction, engineers and contractors have found success by digging deep post holes for foundation supports and filling the hole with many feet of gravel before positioning the posts.

text continues on page 34

LAND OF THE BLUE BISON

IMAGINE SABER-TOOTHED TIGERS, steppe lions, woolly mammoths, and camels living and dying in the place we now call the Tanana Valley. It's a stretch, but evidence of ancient plant life and bones is preserved in the rock record from 100,000 years ago up to 10,000 years ago. Often, parts of prehistoric animals are unearthed.

During the last ice age, the Interior was a glacier-free grassland called a steppe. It was cold and dry, and apparently a refuge for many animals crowded in by glaciation to the north and south. Across the steppe roamed a wide variety of mammals—some now extinct, others early ancestors of animals here today, such as moose, sheep, caribou, musk oxen, ground squirrels, and beavers.

Throughout the Interior, modern earth movers in the form of gold miners, road builders, and archeologists often excavate bones, tusks, fossils, and the like, proof that prehistoric Alaska was nothing like what we see today. Gold miners find pieces of fossilized mammoth tusks so often that the museums turn them away, accepting only the most intact specimens, pieces of ancient ivory that can measure up to 12 feet long.

In one of the most amazing finds of the late 20th century, University of Alaska Fairbanks professor Dale Guthrie uncovered the mummified remains of a steppe bison in 1979. Its hide had turned the color of metallic blue from surrounding minerals, so it was later dubbed "Blue Babe." A nearly complete specimen, the animal was unearthed near a mine site just outside Fairbanks. Following thorough study, Guthrie reported that the mature bull had been killed about 36,000 years ago. Cause of death: 2 or 3 steppe lions. Today, the preserved remains of Blue Babe are on display at the University of Alaska Museum, a testament to another chapter in Alaska's history. ■

*Chief Peter John, the Athabascan traditional chief
of the Tanana Chiefs Conference.*

THE ATHABASCANS

THE ORIGINAL INHABITANTS of Alaska likely migrated into the territory 10,000 to 15,000 years ago over a land bridge that is now submerged beneath the Bering Sea. It once connected Asia with North America, and animals as well as people moved freely between the two continents. Anthropologists are fairly certain that some of those travelers settled in Alaska's Interior while many others splintered off and kept moving south. The proof lies in the language. The Athabascans of Canada and Alaska are linguistically connected to Indians of the southwestern United States. Furthermore, evidence suggests that some of these early ancestors moved on to settle in Central and South America.

Among all of Alaska's Native groups, the Athabascans laid claim to the largest area, and the people were divided into more than a dozen subgroups that spoke different dialects. Trade fairs were common, with great numbers gathered to exchange goods, sing, dance, and feast.

In the Interior, the Athabascans' seminomadic lifestyle matched the rhythms of the seasons. Living off big game, small furbearers, fish, and waterfowl, the first people were accustomed to breaking camp seasonally, sometimes even weekly, to rendezvous with the creatures on which they depended. They dried meat and smoked fish, tanned furs, and made clothing, tents, and blankets from animal skins. Even bones and sinew were used to make useful objects such as eating utensils or sewing needles and thread. Tree bark was made into baskets, bowls, and baby carriers. A lining of moss was an easily replaced diaper.

The ingenious ways in which the Athabascans survived were in stark contrast to the ways of Westerners who started arriving during the mid-1800s. Early settlers arrived with sleds and wagons, metal pots and pans, wool blankets, calico cloth, and canvas tents. Bartering with Russians, Canadians, French, English, and Americans, the Indians traded what they had for beads, flour, sugar, bacon, coffee, fabric, yarn, and tobacco.

Like their ancestors, many modern-day Athabascans tan furs and sew skins into mitts, slippers, and parkas. They snare rabbits for stew, collect eggs, and boil moosehead soup. Along riverbanks, they build ingenious floating fish wheels that use the river's current to turn a log "Ferris wheel" that catches fish effortlessly. Large arms are covered with netting, forming baskets that capture the fish. The arms pull up out of the water as the current propels the wheel. At the apex of the turn, the fish drop into a holding box while the other basket moves underwater, and the cycle repeats. Athabascans still use racks and smokehouses to dry or smoke their salmon. And they dance, sing songs, and ask elders to retell the stories handed down for generations. Yet they also watch satellite television, use high-powered rifles on hunting trips, and wear jeans and T-shirts. Villagers enjoy an occasional trip into Fairbanks to see a movie, eat out, or stock up at the discount food warehouse. The people have survived dramatic change in a short space of time by adopting some Western ways by chance and some by choice. ◼

Ice fog shrouds Fairbanks at minus 50°F.

While ice is ever present below ground, up above there are no glaciers in this region of Alaska, nor have there been for millions of years. Geologists say that Fairbanks and most of Interior Alaska were spared from glaciation during the last ice age. Rather, the region remained a grassland on which animals and people were able to survive. The evidence lies not only in the landscape's appearance, which lacks the scoured features that glaciers leave behind, but also in fossils and artifacts. In fact, some fossils were carbon-dated at between 12,000 and 30,000 years old, indicating certain species that once roamed this valley had survived several ice ages. Among them were mastodons, musk oxen, saber-toothed cats, mammoths, moose, sheep, and even horses.

Archeologists thrilled to find artifacts such as flint blades in the College Hill dig near Fairbanks that closely matched those found in Asia, lending credence to the theory that people migrated here from Asia across the Bering Land Bridge. The finger of land that once connected present-day Siberia with Alaska's Seward Peninsula is now submerged beneath the Bering Sea.

For thousands of years, the Tanana Valley has been a pristine wilderness rich in resources that sustained the indigenous Athabascan Indians. As recently as a century ago, they lived with little concern for the outside world, even though many coastal areas of Alaska had already been visited, explored, and invaded by Westerners, some friendly, but most hostile or indifferent to the Natives. Few Westerners, however, made the effort to reach the great Interior when the sea was so rich with sea otters, fur seals, and whales.

In the Interior, moose, bears, fish, waterfowl, and small furbearers provided sustenance for the Athabascans. The bird and animal bones, sinew, and fur were materials used for clothing, shelter, utensils, and weapons. Today, in the small villages throughout the Interior, Native Alaskans still rely heavily on big game, ducks, geese, fish, and small furbearers to subsist off the land. Many ancient cultural traditions remain alive, handed down from generation to generation.

The first Alaskans, as well as newer, foreign arrivals, followed the major waterways—the Yukon and Tanana Rivers—along with smaller tributaries and overland trails, as transportation corridors. The Athabascans knew the country well, having traveled throughout it and beyond, following their food resources, trading with neighboring tribes, and camping in small, mobile communities. In 1885, Lieutenant Allen was amazed at the accuracy of the hand-drawn maps he received from Athabascans in the Copper River area.

During the late 1800s, the few non-Natives in these parts traded goods, prospected for gold, and brought their own brands of religion, dress, art, music, and vices to the Athabascan people. The first few years of the 20th century, however, would effect great change when a gold rush—another kind of mobile community— arrived in force in the Tanana Valley. ∎

Flora
and Fauna

Alpine meadows, river floodplains, sloughs, ponds, marshes, and rolling hills dotted with forests of spruce, aspen, willow, and birch. The Tanana Valley and its uplands are beautiful and diverse. And at every elevation, they provide nourishing habitat for large and small mammals, many species of fish, and bird populations that wane and surge with the migratory seasons.

To the north and west of the Interior's natural boundaries lie the treeless areas called tundra. But here in the Tanana Valley is the boreal forest known as *taiga*, a Russian word meaning "land of the little sticks." It's a perfect description for much of this countryside. The little sticks may be the small-diameter birch and aspen trees growing in dense forests, or, more likely, the thickets of black spruce trees. At only 6 or 7 feet tall, these unkempt, stunted coniferous trees may be more than two centuries old. White spruce are their healthier cousins, growing in sweeping, dark green patches among the dominant birch and aspen trees.

In the fall, none of the trees in the Fairbanks area turn red. Rather, the hillsides and valley erupt with shades of brilliant yellow and gold, mingled with the greens of the spruce trees. But, under foot, the uncultivated ground cover outside town fairly

Low-bush cranberries ripen amid reindeer lichen.

---■---

explodes with reds, yellows, and oranges. Those low-lying shrubs include scrub willow and alder, berries, prickly rose, and Labrador tea (which Natives brew for a hot drink).

One of the prime reasons Alaska is seen as a national treasure is the opportunity to reenter a wild world that has disappeared in so many other places. The wild animals are not restrained by bars or fences, hand-fed, or cared for by veterinarians. Fish and wildlife managers have, of course, altered the natural course of life and death in certain populations and continue to monitor numbers to ensure that they thrive. For example, if a harsh winter kills an unusually high number of moose, or spring calf survivals are low, biologists may shorten the next fall's hunting season. They also measure population changes and effects within the food chain. Interdependent species increase and decrease depending on factors such as weather, predation, and availability of food. During a "bunny high" (about every 10 to 12 years, when the hare population is abundant), they, in turn, will be plentiful food for wolves, whose numbers therefore will also increase. Consequently, wildlife managers will keep count of the caribou, to ensure that the thriving wolf population doesn't decimate the herds. If the caribou need protection, biologists may temporarily relax wolf-trapping and hunting regulations.

The Athabascan Indians hunted, fished, and trapped with an attitude of thankfulness to the creatures they killed. In their belief system, animals gave themselves to the people to help sustain them. Customs dictated behavior in special cases. A man was not to speak of his hunting as a braggart would; that would be disrespectful. He was not to talk about bears, in particular, or to gaze directly at a bear being hunted. Waste was not tolerated, and all parts of an animal were used, if possible. The Athabascans understood the migration patterns, feeding habits, population densities, reproductive cycles, and mortality of their prey as well or better than many of today's highly educated biologists.

In Fairbanks, as in other Alaska cities, the wildlife does not recognize artificial boundaries created by humans. Moose follow a dry slough into a residential neighborhood; a black bear breaks

HEALING WITH NATIVE PLANTS

FOR CENTURIES, ATHABASCAN INDIAN HEALERS used local plants and trees to make medicines. The raw materials were plentiful and useful for treating ailments such as common colds, infections, or stomachaches. Today, even though every Native village has access to modern Western medical care and drugs, traditional medicines remain an important part of Athabascan homegrown health care. Here are some examples:

- Wild celery is cooked down for the juice, which is used to treat bad colds.

- Cottonwood tree buds are fried in oil and made into a spread, which is applied to a sore to draw out infection.

- Brewed blackberry leaves make a tea that's used to treat diarrhea.

- The jellied insides of a fireweed stem are used as a salve on boils. ■

A bull moose peers through spruce trees.

into garbage cans on the city limits; wolves attack and kill a sled dog on Chena Hot Springs Road. The intrusions are reminders that humans are latecomers. In sharing this place, people must be mindful to put garbage in well-sealed containers, to respect a moose as a wild creature and not try to feed it like a favorite horse, and to understand that birch trees on riverfront property are invitations to beavers.

People spot wildlife most often when they're camping, hiking, hunting, or fishing in this region's recreation areas and parks. Driving along Fairbanks' outlying roads, you may see moose, porcupine, grouse, or ptarmigan. Canoeing or fishing the Chatanika River or Birch Creek, perhaps you'll see a beaver or river otter, or spy a hawk or golden eagle. Hiking in remote areas may bring you into bear country. You might see snowshoe hares or, in rare instances, a wolf or a red fox. Birders can watch for ravens, waterfowl, sandhill cranes, Canada geese, alder flycatchers, Lincoln sparrows, and orange-crowned warblers.

Check with the Alaska Public Lands Information Center at (907) 456-0527 for locations for wildlife watching. (See also companion volumes in the Alaska Pocket Guide series.) Here's a brief list of what you might see around Fairbanks:

MOOSE: Abundant throughout the Interior, the largest member of the deer family supplies meat to Alaska Natives and to urban families who can fill their freezers in one hunting trip. Males grow antlers and can weigh 1,000 to 1,600 pounds; cows range from 800 to 1,200 pounds. The animals feed on willow, birch, and aspen twigs and favor the young, tender shoots. Sometimes you may see moose submerging their heads in ponds to reach the weeds on the bottom. Calves are born in the spring, and twins are not uncommon. The newborns and young animals are prime targets for bears or wolves.

BEHOLD THE RAVEN

AROUND FAIRBANKS, THE RAVEN is one tough bird—it is bigger than some cats and has an array of vocalizations that carry far on the cold winter air. Pitch black, ravens seem most visible against winter white, pecking through garbage bags in pick-up trucks or gazing down from metal light poles that, incredibly, do not freeze their feet. The birds' amazing circulatory system pumps warm blood to their feet and cool blood back to their hearts in side-by-side vessels. The supercooled blood returning from the feet to the heart via one vessel is rewarmed by heat conducted from the other nearby vessel, thus sustaining the body's core temperature. Throughout Alaska, ravens are protected by the federal Migratory Bird Act, even though their migratory patterns may be only 10 to 20 miles. ■

WOLVES: Found in nearly all of Alaska, these animals are wary and beautiful. At 85 to 115 pounds each, males weigh more than females, which can be 10 to 15 pounds lighter. Wolves eat 4 to 7 pounds of food a day and favor young, sick, or injured animals. In packs, however, they can take down a healthy adult caribou or moose. Most often, packs number 5 to 8 animals. Wildlife managers track their numbers, along with those of moose and caribou, to ensure healthy survival rates for prey and predators alike.

LYNX: Imagine a cat the size of a big dog. These shy cats can weigh from 15 to 45 pounds, and most often roam at night. They sport long fur on their faces and black tufts on their ears. Lynx are considered opportunistic feeders, but they most love snowshoe hares; so they're often found in large river valleys where there are plenty of hares. Especially notable are their huge, round feet with thick fur between the pads, protecting them from cold. Consequently they can easily walk on deep snow—just like a human with snowshoes. Rarely seen by urban dwellers, lynx almost never wander into Fairbanks as moose do.

BEAVERS: At 3 to 4 feet long, the beaver is the largest rodent in North America and is abundant throughout the Interior. Beaver fur is thick and shiny. Athabascans often trap beavers for food and for the fur, which is made into warm winter hats and mitts. As vegetarians, beavers favor the bark and leaves of deciduous trees, sedges, and water plants. If approached while swimming, they will slap their tails before diving, to warn others of your presence. Disappointed Fairbanks landowners along the Chena River have watched as beavers decimated their shoreline stands of trees.

RED FOXES: A member of the canine family, the red fox is found throughout Alaska but thrives in the Interior. Living in such a severe climate, the fox produces a thick, plush pelt coveted by trappers and Native skin sewers. Its diet includes berries, insects, eggs, birds, mice, hares, and carrion. And rather than gorge itself, a fox will create a small cache, or storage area, for its food beneath dry grass or leaves, under the snow. The fur of red foxes changes color in various seasons and makes for some of the most beautiful Native-made hats for sale at local stores and craft fairs.

text continues on page 44

THE MUSK OX FARM

MUSK OXEN WERE ONCE NATIVE to Alaska. Indeed, the great, shaggy beings had survived one ice age after the next only to be wiped out during the industrial age, when they were hunted to extinction. However in 1930, a group of wildlife officials decided to change all that. They formulated a plan to reintroduce the species to Alaska, and with a $40,000 appropriation from the federal government, the group purchased 34 young animals captured from remnant herds in Greenland.

The small herd of calves and yearlings traveled 14,000 miles to Fairbanks and settled into corrals at the college's experiment station. Within 4 years, the first musk ox calves were born, and soon the growing herd was ready for transplant to Nunivak Island, a wildlife refuge in southwestern Alaska. From 1936 on, the animals not only survived, but thrived. Forty years later, there were so many on tiny Nunivak that the state approved a regulated hunt to control their numbers and prevent starvation. Descendants of that original herd were placed in other areas of the state as well, and the total statewide population is now close to 3,000.

At the University of Alaska Fairbanks, the Large Animal Research Station continues to raise musk oxen, as well as other arctic big game, for studies on nutrition and physiology. The facility is open to the public, and more than 100,000 people stop by to visit each year. Check with the University of Alaska at (907) 474-7581 for information on visiting the Large Animal Research Station, also known as the Musk Ox Farm. ■

CREAMER'S FIELD

IN 1903, WHILE OTHER MEN SOUGHT WEALTH in gold mining, C. T. Hinckley chose another path. He selected an area across the Chena River and several miles from the center of the new town, cleared it for farmland, and built a successful dairy.

Twenty-five years later, Hinckley sold his operation to a couple with an apt name for dairy farmers: Charlie and Anna Creamer.

GRIZZLY (BROWN) BEARS: Grizzly, or brown, bears are omnivores—they'll eat animals, salmon, berries, sedges, cow parsnip, horsetails, and carrion. Because of the severe Interior climate, grizzlies here are up to a third smaller than their coastal cousins. They may reach 5 to 6 feet tall and weigh about a thousand pounds. Fur color varies from brown to blond, silver-tipped, and gray-brown. Their eyesight is good

Creamer's Dairy became the northernmost milk producer in the country, and each spring and fall its fallow hayfields attracted thousands of migrating birds: sandhill cranes, Canada geese, mallards, pintails, and numerous other waterfowl. As the city crept closer to the Creamers' land, the fields became a favorite area for bird watching, so popular that when the Creamers retired in 1967, area residents refused to let developers turn the fields into a subdivision. Their protest led to what is today known as Creamer's Field Migratory Waterfowl Refuge, managed by the Alaska Department of Fish and Game. The farmhouse and outbuildings, added to the National Register of Historic Places in 1977, lie at the center of 1,770 acres offering habitat for migratory birds and other animals. Moose, snowshoe hares, and foxes are among the year-round residents, along with other birds such as alder flycatchers, Lincoln sparrows, and orange-crowned warblers.

The farmhouse, which was restored in 1991, serves as a visitor center. Naturalists are on site to answer questions, direct visitors to the nature trails, and distribute literature. In winter, the area is popular for snow sports such as snowmobiling, cross-country skiing, dog mushing, and ski-joring, in which a skier is pulled by one or two sled dogs. Bow hunting and trapping are permitted in certain areas of the refuge.

Most often, visitors come to walk the nature trails and glass the hayfields, to quietly watch the feeding geese and cranes and read the interpretive signs. Creamer's Field is located at 1300 College Road, between downtown Fairbanks and the University of Alaska. For information, call the Farmhouse Visitor Center at (907) 459-7307. ■

but not great; however, their senses of hearing and scent are excellent. Given the chance, they'd rather leave than confront; however, they will attack to protect their cubs or a kill. Winter denning in the Interior is almost half the year, from late October through April or May. Cubs are born in the den in midwinter, and the drowsy mother nurses and keeps them warm until spring.

A Toklat grizzly bear.

BLACK BEARS: Some people have trouble distinguishing between a dark grizzly and a black bear in a brown color phase. Generally, black bears are much smaller, weighing from 100 to 200 pounds. They also have a smaller head in proportion to body size. They lack the typical dished-snout profile of the grizzly and its distinctive shoulder humps. Local black bears eat berries, tender green vegetation, fresh meat, and carrion. Garbage is attractive to them, too. Black bears can effortlessly climb trees. They spend nearly half the year in the den—from October to April or May, but don't really hibernate. Instead, they doze the winter away and can be awakened easily.

Because Fairbanks is an urban island surrounded by wilderness, the phrase "balance of nature" is especially appropriate. To borrow from the police motto, "To Preserve and Protect" is among the primary responsibilities of the humans who share this place with wildlife. It applies to those who hunt, trap, and fish, as well as to those who prefer to shoot wildlife with their cameras. Native and non-Native alike, the people of the Interior continue to honor and uphold the balance. ■

Gold and a
Pioneer Town

This is it? We're getting off here?

Elbridge Truman "E. T." Barnette stood on the deck of the stern-wheeler *Lavelle Young,* angry and disgusted, staring at a muddy riverbank with nothing but birch and spruce beyond it. Arguing and beseeching the captain to push up the Chena River had proven useless. Thwarted by low water, Captain Charles Adams had backtracked a few miles, stopped, and told Barnette to get off the boat. It was August 26, 1901. A party of men from the boat would help to cut timber and build a shelter quickly before the stern-wheeler departed. Snow would be arriving in a few short weeks.

This was not going according to Barnette's plan, but the plan had changed several times already. He'd recently suffered a great financial loss when an inexperienced crew member cracked up his own vessel, the *Arctic Boy,* at St. Michael even before he could get started up the Yukon River. Already in debt, Barnette had signed another note to get his trade goods onto the *Lavelle Young.*

An entrepreneur named John Jerome Healy had strongly urged Barnette to open a trading post on the upper Tanana River at Tanana Crossing, now called Tanacross. Barnette had Healy's grandiose assurances that he himself would build a railroad

A paddle-wheeler still plies the Chena and Tanana Rivers.

———■———

*By 1904, the Chena River waterfront bloomed
into a commerce center.*

---

between mining camps at Valdez and Eagle that would intersect
with Barnette's post, thus guaranteeing heavy business.

Things went wrong again for Barnette in this foray up the Chena
River following the tip of an Indian who said the "Rock River" was a
shortcut around a difficult stretch of the Tanana. The captain of the
Lavelle Young, with its 3-foot draft, refused to risk grounding in the
shallow waters ahead. Neither would he take a fully loaded vessel
back downstream with inadequate steam power to work against the
current should they become stuck on a sand bar. Barnette had no
choice but to get off the boat in the middle of nowhere, with almost
no chance of getting any customers all winter long.

Barnette, his wife Isabelle, and several men he had employed,
along with $20,000 worth of supplies—food, tools, hardware,
doors, windows, a dog team, even a horse—were off-loaded to the

banks of the Chena River in a spot near today's Cushman Street Bridge. Their hopes dashed for the year, they planned to spend the winter there and then go south in the spring, secure another flat-bottomed boat, retrieve their supplies, and continue to Tanana Crossing. That was the plan, at least.

As upset and disappointed as he was, Barnette had no idea that the plume of steam created by the riverboat was visible many miles away in the surrounding hills, and that it had been spotted by a gold miner named Felix Pedro, who was low on supplies. Hoping to restock for the winter, Pedro and his partner, Tom Gilmore, began the 15-mile trek toward the sign of civilization. Barnette's first customers showed up within 12 hours of landing.

So far, Pedro had been an unlucky miner, working the hills for years and occasionally finding "color," some evidence of gold, but never getting rich. There was the unhappy time in 1898 when he thought he'd struck it, then later could not find the stream again. When Pedro met Barnette, neither man was feeling very lucky. But soon all that would change.

Barnette was a well-traveled man with a poor reputation, especially on the Yukon River at Circle City, where he gouged the miners and trappers during his virtual monopoly on supplies. Not content to spend his years trading flour for furs in an out-of-the-way spot, Barnette was in it only for the money.

The following spring, the Barnette party did make it back to Seattle, where he obtained more credit, added to his supplies, and arranged for a boat to be shipped to Nome in pieces; he would assemble it there. Aboard his new vessel, dubbed the *Isabelle*, Barnette returned to the camp on the Chena River (or at least close to it—the *Isabelle* was unable to come upriver even as far as the *Lavelle Young* had). It was early September when he arrived to hear the big news, already more than a month old: on July 22, 1902, Felix Pedro had struck gold.

Instantly Barnette went out to the creeks and began staking claims willy-nilly for himself and every relative for whom he had power of attorney. Of course he would stay now, for soon the stampede would come to him. He would become a wealthy man, and later mayor of a town that quickly sprang up around the trading post.

AGRICULTURE THEN AND NOW

DESPITE ITS NORTHERN LATITUDE and short growing season, the Tanana Valley is exceptionally fertile, as the early settlers discovered. The trick was knowing what to plant, for only the hardiest strains would thrive.

In the early 1920s, the Tanana Valley was the most extensively developed agricultural area in Alaska. Blessed with a generous

A fateful meeting with Federal District Judge James Wickersham during Barnette's return trip in the fall of 1902 had inspired him to name the town Fairbanks, at the judge's request. The concept of friends in high places suited Barnette. He saw the benefit in a handshake agreement with Wickersham, and Wickersham wanted to honor Charles W. Fairbanks, then a U.S. senator from Indiana. By 1904, Fairbanks was vice president of the United States under Teddy Roosevelt, no doubt a pleasing

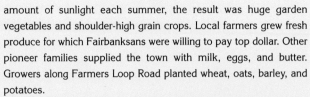

amount of sunlight each summer, the result was huge garden vegetables and shoulder-high grain crops. Local farmers grew fresh produce for which Fairbanksans were willing to pay top dollar. Other pioneer families supplied the town with milk, eggs, and butter. Growers along Farmers Loop Road planted wheat, oats, barley, and potatoes.

In 1924, farming leaders formed the Tanana Valley Fair Association, and the tradition of the Tanana State Fair, Alaska's oldest fair, carries on today, with a week of festivities in early August. A perennial favorite is the competition for the biggest cabbage, a whopping 40 pounds in 1999. The fairgrounds are located along College Road at Aurora Drive; call (907) 452-3750 for more information.

All summer long, visitors and locals alike relish the Farmer's Market, located near the entrance of the fairgrounds. Open on Wednesdays and Saturdays from May through September, the Farmer's Market features produce from local farms, along with handmade crafts and knickknacks; call (907) 456-3276 for more information.

Founded in 1906, the Agriculture Experiment Station off Tanana Drive on the university campus is an active component of UAF's research and teaching programs. Some 260 acres of land are devoted to crops and another 50 acres to forestry research and demonstration. At the nearby Georgeson Botanical Garden, tours are available between May and September from 8 A.M. to 7 P.M. daily. Visitors may wander among the perennial and herb gardens, along a boreal-forest nature trail, and through the vegetable and fruit demonstration garden. A small visitors center offers publications on the joys and challenges of northern gardening. ∎

development for Wickersham. What's more, Barnette's favor-for-a-favor association with Wickersham ensured that, if the little town was named Fairbanks, it would flower. The powerful judge promised to move the seat of the Third Judicial District Court from Eagle to Fairbanks.

The miners who came to Fairbanks were experienced men who had followed the gold rush from Juneau to Circle City, the Klondike, and Nome. They knew one another, and some wrote that

CHENA HOT SPRINGS

IN 1910, THE POPULATION of Fairbanks was 3,541, but another 7,500 miners lived on their claims throughout the area. Chena Hot Springs became a premier getaway, both for city folk and the miners whose labor-intensive work drove them to the soothing waters of the hot mineral springs. A bath was only 50 cents back then. At just over 60 miles from town, Chena was a 2-day trip by horse-drawn sleigh or wagon for Fairbanksans.

Although Athabascans had long enjoyed these springs, and others at Manley and Circle, Chena Hot Springs was "discovered" by brothers Robert and Thomas Swan in 1905. The water flowed from the ground at 156°F and had to be cooled for the soaking pools. By 1920, under new management, it was a full-fledged spa with grounds that included a grocery store, hotel, men's clothing store, and a dozen log cabins renting for $20 a month. Inside the main log bathhouse, 4 log- and stone-lined tubs were available for bathing. Visitors could opt to lie on a stone pad in a floorless sweat room as steam rose from the rocky soil.

Today the resort is little more than an hour's drive from Fairbanks at the dead end of Chena Hot Springs Road. Combining rustic décor and surroundings with modern conveniences, the resort features a restaurant-bar, glassed-in pool, outdoor hot tubs, cross-country skiing, snowmobiling, horse-drawn sleigh rides, and a cabin for viewing the northern lights. Visitors can reserve a rustic cabin or stay in a modern hotel room. For more information, call (907) 452-7867. ■

the faces seemed so familiar that it was as if they were back in Dawson, in the Klondike rush of '98. But there was a difference here. Miners and merchants had tired of going it alone, and they sent for their wives and families to join them. Women and children, wallpaper and calico, churches and reading rooms all contributed to the sense that this place would last.

While area Athabascans had always hunted and fished in the Tanana Valley, they had never settled permanently at the river's edge, but rather lived in seasonal camps. Two miles away, where the University of Alaska Fairbanks now stands atop College Hill, was a site often used by the ancient Athabascans. In the early 1900s, most Interior Natives knew of the strangers' settlement on the banks of the Chena, but chose to avoid it. They carried on as they'd always lived. Those who were willing or simply curious occasionally walked for many miles to the town to trade furs for food, tobacco, cookware, or Western-style clothing. Some served as expert guides or advisors.

Meanwhile, Fairbanks continued to grow. Within a few years, Barnette was the mayor of a full-fledged town with all the amenities and vices common to frontier communities: Fourth of July parades and tug-of-wars on First Avenue, prostitution on Third, 33 saloons in the space of 4 blocks, a lending library, churches, concerts, and plays. Records show that by 1910, almost $30 million in gold was taken from Interior creeks. Between regular, guarded shipments of gold to Seattle, the Washington–Alaska Bank vault was overflowing with gold, and commerce was often conducted with gold dust, not greenbacks.

By March 1911, some shady dealings by Barnette with the Washington–Alaska Bank created a situation in which he had to steal away from Fairbanks under cover of darkness. Later he would be charged with embezzling $317,000. The original Teflon-coated criminal, he was found guilty of only one misdemeanor in a trial that angry Fairbanksans termed "a mockery of justice." In the *News-Miner,* a new term for theft was coined: "you've just been Barnetted." Afterward, Barnette flitted between Mexico and southern California, speculating and losing money. Isabelle took their two daughters and left him in 1920, citing infidelity.

FINDING ALASKA'S HIDDEN TREASURE

SO WHY IS THE GOLD HERE and not in, say, Kansas? Interior Alaska as we know it was once a part of the British Columbia coast. Geologically split from the mainland by the Tintina Fault, the section moved slowly northward over the space of 100 million years. Today's Tanana Valley was underlain by a metamorphic rock called Birch Creek schist, which played a significant role in the formation of gold deposits even while this part of Alaska was much farther south.

From 145 to 85 million years ago, molten igneous rocks from deep within the earth moved upward into the Birch Creek schist, bringing with it superheated vapor-liquid that held dissolved gold. As the vapor-liquid moved away from the magma, changes in pressure and temperature altered the fluid's chemistry, and gold was deposited either in veins or as particles trapped within the igneous rock. Those are two ways that gold can be found today. Gold deposited in veins is mined in underground tunnels, and gold particles in granite are recovered by pulverizing the rock and using chemicals to dissolve the gold so that it can be concentrated.

A third type of gold deposit is called "placer" (pronounced *plă-sir*) gold. As the rock around it eroded, the heavy gold, combined with the sand and gravel, was washed down the rivers and became concentrated

The bizarre story of the town's beginnings adds dimension to the names on street signs and geographical features: Pedro Dome and Wickersham Dome in the Tanana Hills, Barnette Street in the downtown street grid, Isabel Pass in the Alaska Range, and Wickersham Hall on the university campus.

However, none of the principals of that early drama are buried in the city they helped birth. Felix Pedro's health was poor even as he made his big strike. As a rich man, he found a wife and toured Europe before returning to Alaska. He died at age 52 on July 22,

in the base of streambeds—those that still exist and those that have been buried for thousands of years. It's the most prevalent type of gold deposit in the Interior, and the kind that Felix Pedro discovered.

Water is essential for separating placer gold from the overburden (the soil and gravel around it). In some places, miners used high-pressure water run through an apparatus called a "giant" to wash away the overburden on entire hillsides.

Drift mining was another common method. In winter months, miners built fires on the ground to thaw it. They'd remove the resulting mud and build another fire, repeating the process until they'd reached the "pay dirt"—the layer of gravel and muck in which the gold was found—which they set aside until summer, when they could run water through the pay dirt in their sluice box and wash the gold out.

In the 1930s and '40s, the Fairbanks Exploration Company extracted gold with floating dredges, multistory gold-processing ships. A conveyor belt of buckets chewed at the ground in front of the dredge and brought the rock and soil inside, where the gold was sorted out and the gravel "tailings" were tossed out the back. Gold Dredge No. 8, off the Steese Highway north of Fairbanks, is the only one of the retired dredges open for tours.

No matter how it is mined, gold claims a hold over the finder. Gold miners understand its monetary value, but many speak of another thrill they experience when they find it. Their hearts quicken, knowing they are the first to touch something that has never been seen by the human eye, something that was formed perhaps 100 million years ago. ■

1910—8 years to the day after his discovery—and was buried in San Francisco. E. T. Barnette was 70 in 1933 when he died in Los Angeles after suffering a skull fracture in a fall. Wickersham was 82, blind, and nearly bankrupt when he died in Juneau in October 1939 and was buried in Tacoma, Washington.

The intersection of these three unique lives—the wheeler-dealer, the judge, and the hard-working immigrant—had put Fairbanks on the map. ■

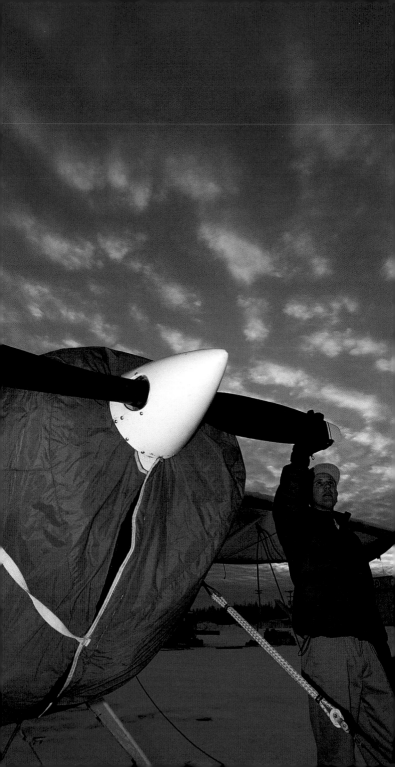

From Aviation Experiments to War, and Statehood

Had E. T. Barnette been a stellar citizen and retired comfortably in the town he founded, he would have delighted in the next big development in frontier Fairbanks: aviation. More likely, he would have traded stock in the first airlines.

In the 1920s and '30s, early Fairbanks aviators such as Carl Ben Eielson, Noel Wein, Joe Crosson, and Harold Gillam were truly seat-of-the-pants fliers, for flight in the deep cold and on undeveloped airstrips of the Far North was an experimental proposition. Crashes were as common, it seemed, as takeoffs. And yet airplane travel at once expanded the horizons and shortened distances for mail and freight delivery all over the territory. Soon aircraft took over the work of men who for decades had followed the "mail trails," driving freight and mail by dog team and draft horse. As a growing town in a central location, Fairbanks quickly evolved into an aviation hub and, in August 1935, welcomed celebrities Will Rogers and Wiley Post during a stopover on their fatal flight to Barrow.

The Alaska Railroad, begun in 1915, connected the great Interior with the town of Seward on the southcentral coast of Alaska, making trans-Alaska travel all the more convenient. President Warren G. Harding visited the Interior in 1923 to drive the

Bob Bursiel, owner of Wright Air Service, completes a flight check.

■

"golden spike" in Nenana connecting the railroad's northern and southern portions.

By the 1930s, Fairbanks' social life settled into a pleasant routine of plays, musical concerts, ladies' teas, and winter sports contests between the boys in town and up at College. The annual Winter Carnival featured curling, dog mushing, and ice skating on the Chena River. In summer, families enjoyed picnics at Harding Lake, excursions to Chena Hot Springs, and viewing the farmers' giant cabbage entries in the Tanana Valley Fair. The water delivery-man came around in every season, and everybody, it seemed, had electric lights.

The 1940s were years of great transformation in the Interior, a decade in which the population more than doubled. On April 14, 1940, Ladd Airfield opened adjacent to Fairbanks. The decision to build an airfield in this remote frontier town was a timely one. With the bombing of Pearl Harbor on December 7, 1941, Ladd became a strategic site in the Allies' northern defense. A flurry of military activity ensued, including the creation of the Northwest Staging Route in 1942. Composed of a string of airfields from Great Falls, Montana, through

"PARAPUPS" SEARCH AND RESCUE

DURING WORLD WAR II, Ladd Airfield was also home to another kind of soldier. The Veterinary Section, Service Command, Alaska Defense Command maintained a kennel of parachuting search-and-rescue dogs called "parapups." Along with a musher, a surgeon, and at least 2 other enlisted men, the dogs parachuted from about 1,500 feet in singles or pairs with cargo parachutes attached to heavy, well-padded harnesses. Stationed at Fairbanks, Anchorage, and Nome, plus a handful of bases in western Canada, 29 dog teams were in service by the end of the war. Rescue operations by sled dog had dramatically improved the survival odds for stranded and injured soldiers before the use of helicopters. ■

The Co-Op, a local landmark and gathering place downtown.

western Canada, the route terminated at Ladd. Over this route, pilots delivered nearly 8,000 lend-lease program warplanes bound for Russia.

In the mid-1940s, Fairbanks was crawling with Russian pilots and crew who loved to buy American souvenirs at Piggly-Wiggly, Samson Hardware, and other local shops. At the peak of the lend-lease program, a hundred fighters, bombers, and cargo planes per month were turned over to the Russian pilots to complete their journey across the Bering Sea. Some of the lend-lease pilots were women, who were then not permitted to fly in combat. Two of them, Celia Hunter and Ginny Wood, have made their home in Fairbanks since their lend-lease days.

Ladd also became the site of the Army Cold Weather Test Station where anything soldiers might use in a high-latitude war—such as clothing, machinery motor oil, and gun workings—was tested in the subarctic environment.

Fairbanks boomed in the shower of defense spending, and civil-service jobs often paid two to three times better than other available jobs. Additional jobs opened up when the government

SANTA CLAUS HOUSE

Most children only dream of visiting Santa Claus House. The kids in North Pole, Alaska, population 1,619, are neighbors.

A beloved institution, Santa Claus House lies 14 miles southeast of Fairbanks on the Richardson Highway. You can't miss it—it's the only red-and-white place with two Gulliver-size Santas in the yard. Inside is a combination toy store, gift shop, and throne room for Santa. Founded in 1952 by the

original Mr. and Mrs. Claus, Con and Nellie Miller, the store is operated today by their children and grandchildren.

Even though about 95 percent of letters to Santa are handled at local post offices, each year about 20,000 Christmas letters make it through to the North Pole Post Office. Another 300,000 letters are pre-addressed Christmas cards to be canceled with the North Pole, Alaska, stamp. Volunteers and extra employees help the postmaster at Christmastime.

North Pole was incorporated in 1952 on former homestead land. Conveniently located between the two military installations, many subdivided lots were purchased by military families, and soon the town took shape.

A tree-lighting ceremony in early December is an annual civic highlight kicking off the Christmas season. And on the flip side of the year, the crowds cheer when Santa appears in July's Golden Days Parade, waving from atop the North Pole Fire Department's ladder truck. ■

decided to build an overland route connecting the Lower 48 with Alaska. The ALCAN (the Alaska-Canada Highway) was hurriedly constructed and roughly connected the "dots" of the Northwest Staging Route airfields. Completing their job in a matter of months, 10,000 soldiers and 6,000 civilians labored to build the 1,671-mile road through some of the most rugged country on the continent and in horrendous conditions. An amazing engineering accomplishment, even today, the road officially opened on November 20, 1942.

As the war intensified, in 1943 the government constructed Eielson Air Force Base on land 30 miles south of Fairbanks. By war's end, the Civil Aeronautics Administration and the U.S. Army and Navy had spent more than $400 million on developing the country's northern air defenses in Alaska.

After the war, both Ladd Field (later renamed Fort Wainwright) and Eielson continued to grow and became an important part of the Fairbanks landscape, social life, and economic base. Military spending increased during the establishment of programs to protect the country with the Distant Early Warning system (DEW Line), and White Alice radar sites.

However, gone was the Fairbanks that old-timers fondly remembered. A boom in housing, communications, and transportation had altered the small-town atmosphere. Thousands more new faces crowded the streets, and with the 1950s came eventful changes that would spur yet another growth spurt: statehood.

Not everyone was in favor of joining the union, and serious talks on statehood had been placed on the back burner several times since 1944. But those who were in favor had powerful voices: Territorial Governor Ernest Gruening, Delegate Bob Bartlett, and future governor Bill Egan, along with newspapermen such as *The Anchorage Times* publisher Bob Atwood and, in Fairbanks, C. W. "Bill" Snedden, publisher of the *Fairbanks Daily News-Miner.* Finally Alaska adopted the "Tennessee Plan," a clever strategy used by proponents of statehood for Tennessee whereby they got a foot in the door of

text continues on page 66

UNIVERSITY OF ALASKA FAIRBANKS

JUDGE JAMES WICKERSHAM gets credit for helping found America's "Farthest North College," as it was once nicknamed. The question is, when was it founded?

The Alaska Agricultural College and School of Mines officially opened in 1922, but the ceremony to lay a cornerstone had occurred in 1917. With no forthcoming funds to actually build the school, Wickersham was intent on keeping the concept alive in the minds of Fairbanks' residents and before Congress.

Over its long and illustrious history, the college, which later became the University of Alaska Fairbanks, has changed the date on its official seal from 1922 (when it opened) to 1935 (when it became a university) to 1917 (when the AACSM was incorporated).

The 2,250-acre site on College Hill placed the school several miles away from the Fairbanks city center, and the community around it was actually called College. In the first few years, the handful of Alaskan students—both men and women—lived in cabins on homesteads nearby or took the train to the one-room train station at the foot of the hill. Mining, agriculture, and home economics were among the earliest fields of study.

World War II virtually gutted the young faculty and student body, but the university's president, Charles Bunnell, was determined to keep the school open. A decade later, the university became the site of the Constitutional Convention, where delegates from around the state met to hammer out the important document on the road to statehood. Today's bookstore and post office are now housed in Constitution Hall, where the document was drafted.

The university now has its own fire station, medical facility, radio and television stations, and concert hall. Its library is the repository for a wealth of historical documents and photographs relating to the Far North. It has developed a reputation as a leading school for the hard sciences, among them geology, geophysics, arctic biology, and aurora research. At Poker Flats, a satellite site near the old Chatanika gold camp on the Steese Highway, rocket research is conducted. And on campus, the University of Alaska Museum is today recognized for its outstanding displays and collections of gold and archeological finds.

In 1991, Congress appointed $25 million to fund a supercomputer center in Alaska, and the Fairbanks campus was chosen as the site. The Arctic Region Supercomputing Center now houses the most powerful computer in the state, a $10.2 million CRAY supercomputer that is 50,000 times more powerful than the average desktop computer. The research emphasis of its users, locally and worldwide via the Internet, is science and engineering at high latitudes, especially in the Arctic.

Over the years, many thousands of students have filed through the university's degree programs, among them former governor Jay Hammond and famed environmentalist Margaret Murie, author of the Alaska classic *Two in the Far North* (see "Recommended Reading"). Today, the university continues to shine as an outpost of academia. ■

Austin E. Lathrop   *Augie Hiebert*

EARLY MEDIA STARS

AUSTIN E. "CAP" LATHROP was Alaska's first media mogul and the prime mover in modernizing Fairbanks. In the 1930s, he owned the *Fairbanks Daily News-Miner* and started the town's first radio station, KFAR. Lathrop also built several beautifully appointed movie theaters in the state, each of them an "Empress Theatre," including the Empress in Fairbanks, built in 1927. It was the first building in Fairbanks to be made of reinforced concrete, and naysayers said it would crumble in the freeze and thaw. The building still stands on Second Avenue, where, after a long midlife as the Co-op

Congress: they simply sent a delegation to D.C. to act as unofficial congresspeople representing their "state."

In Fairbanks, Bill Snedden's local campaign was equally clever. Since so many residents were newcomers to the area, courtesy of Uncle Sam, he urged them to contact their home-state lawmakers and lobby for statehood. If the letter writers received a positive response, Snedden ran their pictures in the paper. Also, using his talent for reporting, Snedden created a card file with private "gossipy" information on each U.S. legislator that some say helped influence votes.

Fairbanks Daily News-Miner

C.W. "Bill" Snedden

Drugstore, it was renovated into a mini-mall during the early 1990s.

Broadcaster Augie Hiebert came to Fairbanks in 1939. He and his dog, Sparky, were on-air celebrities at KFAR radio, where Hiebert read birthday wishes and other greetings, and Sparky barked on command. In December 1941, Hiebert was scanning the short-wave bands before his morning shift when he learned that Pearl Harbor had been bombed. The first in Fairbanks to hear the news—even before the military radio operators at nearby Ladd Field—he broadcast it to his listeners. Hiebert would later take the helm at KFAR and build a chain of radio and television stations throughout the state.

Publisher of the *Fairbanks Daily News-Miner* from 1950 until his death in 1989, C. W. "Bill" Snedden was a leader in helping to achieve statehood through his editorials and personal influence. When the Constitutional Convention delegates met at the University of Alaska in 1955–56, Snedden, lacking a telephone connection with the school, personally strung telephone wire in the trees for 2 miles so that he could provide up-to-date reports for his readers. ■

Congress passed the statehood measure on June 30, 1958, and Bill Snedden and his staff hustled to print a special statehood edition of the paper, then flew it south to ensure that every congressperson received a copy on July 1. He was determined to prove that Fairbanks was no backwater. In the Tanana Valley, people celebrated their new status with bonfires, in bars, and in a failed attempt to dye the Chena River gold.

On January 3, 1959, President Dwight D. Eisenhower signed the statehood proclamation. Alaska became the 49th star. ■

Disaster, Then
the Biggest Boom

Given its recovery from repeated catastrophes, Fairbanks might well have been nicknamed the "Bounce-Back City" instead of the "Golden Heart City."

Even as early as 1906, when fire swept through the log-cabin town, mill operators were selling lumber to rebuild before the ashes had cooled, and the bars were doing business again within 24 hours. Later, Fairbanks weathered the alleged banking improprieties of its founding father, E. T. Barnette, who slipped out of town with full pockets. People watched the mining industry boom with soaring gold prices, only to slip back again during downturns in the market. Military spending in the 1940s and '50s fueled the economy and kept Fairbanks alive, but the drain on the town through leaps in population was dizzying. Would the ups and downs ever level out?

And then, in August 1967, just as the state was celebrating the 100th anniversary of Alaska's transfer from Russia to the United States, disaster struck once more. At the end of a wet summer came a week of inch-a-day rainfall, and the Chena River crested 6 feet above its banks, driving people from their homes. More than 7,000 people found shelter well above the floodwaters at the University of Alaska Fairbanks, camping in buildings

The Chena River left its banks in 1967.

ALASKALAND

IN THE MID-1960s, civic leaders decided that constructing a pioneer park seemed a fitting way to celebrate the 100th anniversary of Alaska's transfer from Russia to the United States, and thus the 44-acre Alaskaland was born. Opened in 1967 under the mantle of the Alaska '67 Exposition, the park plays out Alaska's history in theme areas, including a Gold Rush Town, an area devoted to gold-mining history, life-size replicas of Native dwellings, room for playgrounds and picnic areas, a central building to include art exhibit areas and a theater, and the crown jewel: the riverboat SS *Nenana*, one of the last working stern-wheelers, which retired to this park.

designated as fallout shelters and forming sandbag brigades trying to protect the university's new power plant near the foot of College Hill.

Although records show that Fairbanks suffered $200 million in damage, this figure does not include the loss of priceless family and archival treasures—photo albums, letters, collections, and

In the 30-plus years since the park was constructed, Alaskaland has become a symbol of this city—diverse and enduring. A narrow-gauge railroad on an elevated track encircles the park. A number of Fairbanks' earliest buildings were relocated to Gold Rush Town and restored into mini-museums and shops. Some—like the old church, the Pantages Theater, and the Palace Saloon—are still living out their original use. Judge James Wickersham's home is here and, scandalously close by, several of the cabins from the infamous Fairbanks "Line," a street set apart for prostitution.

The Pioneers of Alaska Museum contains a collection of artifacts, paintings, and photos donated by local pioneers. At one end of the building's exterior, a sign marks the water line of the 1967 flood, a natural catastrophe that occurred in the same year that the park opened. Near the main entrance is the Harding Car, the luxury railroad car that President Warren G. Harding used during his visit in 1923. And over in the Mining Valley are antique, weathered mining machinery and the outdoor grills of the Alaska Salmon Bake restaurant.

The SS *Nenana,* restored to its glory days, holds center stage next to the Alaskaland Civic Center. Visitors are welcome to explore the stern-wheeler or check out the latest art or theater offerings at the civic center.

Alaskaland is a popular attraction for first-time visitors, as well as a favorite place for locals to spend their leisure time. Admission is free, and the park is located on Airport Way at Peger Road. For information on summertime activities, call (907) 459-1095. ■

The historic riverboat, SS Nenana, *drydocked in Alaskaland.*

■

important documents—that were destroyed in the flood. A personal history of Fairbanks remains forever lost.

With Fairbanks officially designated a disaster area, residents soon received federal assistance to rebuild, which they did with vigor. A year later, the little town on the banks of the Chena River was named an "All-American City" by the National Civic League.

ALASKA NATIVE CLAIMS SETTLEMENT

UNRESOLVED DECISIONS about land ownership came to a head during the planning of the trans-Alaska pipeline. Who owned the land in the pipeline corridor? From as far back as 1867, when the United States acquired Alaska from Russia, all the way to statehood in 1959, the U.S. government had put off making final determination of Alaska Native rights to lands. Many miles of the pipeline would pass through what had traditionally been Athabascan homeland; however, the indigenous people could not claim rights that had not yet been granted to them.

Finally, in 1971, the passage of the Alaska Native Claims Settlement Act settled the issue of Native lands. In the legislation, the U.S. government traded 44 million acres of land and $962.5 million with Alaska Natives in exchange for putting to rest all outstanding aboriginal land claims. Thirteen Native regional corporations were established, along with more than 200 village corporations, and suddenly thousands of people in tiny villages well off the road system were thrust into the world of high finance. Because they lived in a state with tremendous oil and mineral wealth, the people were pressed into a transition from a subsistence economy, in which dollars held less value than food, into a cash economy. Now they were shareholders.

Interior Athabascans formed Doyon Limited as their regional corporation. It continues to manage land and money, plus a broad portfolio of investments to benefit its shareholders, which, as of early 1999, numbered 14,000 people. In the previous fiscal year, Doyon ranked fourth among the 13 Native corporations for gross revenues, earning $70.99 million. ∎

In the years that followed, the Army Corps of Engineers designed and built the Chena River Flood Control Project with a series of gates to redirect rising river water and thus avoid a repeat of the 1967 catastrophe.

Meanwhile, events in the Far North were playing out to Fairbanks' advantage with the discovery of a vast oil reserve in

A homestead north of Fairbanks.

Prudhoe Bay. Alyeska Pipeline Service Company selected Fairbanks for its headquarters, and the company and its contractors spent money generously over the next 2 years. Between 1967 and 1969, the population of Fairbanks surged from 40,000 to 65,000.

But that was nothing compared to what was to come in the next decade: construction of the trans-Alaska pipeline, with Fairbanks as the center of operations for Alyeska and most of the 2,000 contractors and subcontractors who worked on the project. Suddenly Fairbanks was dealing with a crushing influx of people, along with the social ills and economic woes that strike a small town ill prepared to deal with such an enormous project.

Barriers in the form of environmental challenges and questions of land ownership delayed the project, but planning and design moved forward. By the time actual construction began in 1974, the first shipment of pipe had been sitting in a Fairbanks storage yard for 5 years.

From 1969 until the pipeline's completion in 1977, some 70,000 men and women entered the pipeline work force and helped construct the 800-mile tube for transporting crude oil from Alaska's North Slope to the ice-free port of Valdez on Prince William Sound. The Haul Road was also hurriedly built along the pipeline right-of-way, connecting Prudhoe with the existing road system at a spot just north of Fairbanks. In the Lower 48 states, where people railed against sitting in gas lines, there was a sense of urgency for America to tap its own resources.

Across the state, from north to south between Prudhoe and Valdez, 29 pipeline camps sheltered and fed small armies of workers. Many came from Texas, Oklahoma, Louisana, and other oil-producing states. There were Alaska Natives, blacks, whites, Asians, and Latinos. Men and women, educated and uneducated, maids, welders, cooks, and dirtpushers.

The people who worked on the pipeline or who weathered those years in Fairbanks have war stories to tell, just as those pioneers who flooded the Klondike a century ago shared stories of the crazed inflation, lawlessness, and passion of the gold rush of 1898. In Fairbanks, strangers crowded the streets, stores, banks, and post office. The cost of buying meat, milk, and bread skyrocketed. An apartment was almost impossible to find, and landlords jacked up existing rents. Second Avenue was no longer a typical small-town street, but had transformed into vice central, with gambling, prostitution, and free-flowing liquor. The police force was overextended, as were the telephone lines and other utilities.

Some Fairbanksans wondered if they shouldn't just up and leave . . . if the money weren't so good. Along with outsiders, many locals cashed in on the excess of the pipeline wages. In some cases, the sons and daughters of university professors were taking pipeline jobs after high school graduation and making more money than their parents.

Normalcy didn't return to Fairbanks after the first barrel of oil reached Valdez on July 28, 1977. The job market dropped out, and inflated prices for rent, food, and gas remained grossly high compared to like-size communities in the Lower 48. Even today, more than 20 years later, the cost of living remains high. When the

*Nearly half of the trans-Alaska pipeline lies atop
vertical supports; the remainder is buried.*

Alaska Department of Labor published the results of a national survey to determine the most expensive places to live in the country, of the top 10 cities with the highest cost of living, 4 were in Alaska: Kodiak, Juneau, Anchorage, and Fairbanks.

Since the arrival of the first barrel of oil in Valdez in 1977, more than 12 billion barrels of oil have moved through the pipeline. It remains an engineering marvel that was built in virtually untested arctic and subarctic conditions. Some 380 miles of pipe were buried underground in sections where permafrost was less of a concern. The rest is above ground on elevated H-shaped supports. Where the pipe meets the crossbar, it is attached to a Teflon-coated shoe that free-floats on another Teflon shoe, allowing the pipe to move slightly to the left or right without damage if the ground shifts, or when the metal expands and contracts during freezes and

PIPELINE FACTS

- **Length:** 800.3 miles, from Prudhoe Bay south to Valdez, crossing 2 major mountain ranges, 34 major rivers, and 800 smaller streams.

- **Time to complete:** 3 years, 2 months.

- **Cost:** $8 billion in mid-1970s' dollars. In today's dollars, more than $25 billion.

- **Pipeline dimensions:** Pipe is ¹/₂-inch thick with 3.75 inches of insulation on elevated sections. Diameter is 48 inches. Weighs 235 pounds per linear foot.

- **Workers:** From 1969 to 1977, about 70,000; peak employment was 28,072 in October 1975. Five to 10 percent were women.

- **Construction camps:** 29. Largest pipeline camp (1,652 beds) was at Isabel Pass in the Alaska Range.

- **Length of elevated pipe:** Sections totaling 420 miles, requiring some 78,000 H-shaped steel supports, of which 61,000 were equipped with heat pipes to keep the permafrost-riddled soil frozen beneath the supports.

- **Length of buried pipe:** Sections totaling 380 miles, all lying at least 3 feet underground.

- **Haul road:** Supply and service road paralleling the pipeline is 358 miles long and was built in 154 days. Now named the Dalton Highway; open to the public.

- **Average speed of oil:** 5 to 6 miles per hour.

- **Highest point:** Atigun Pass, at 4,739 feet in the Brooks Range.

- **Number of animal crossings constructed:** 579.

- **Valdez terminal:** Holding capacity of 9.18 million barrels. ▪

thaws. At the top of each support column, engineers have erected long wands of narrow, metal fins that connect with posts deep in the ground. In permafrost areas, the fins act as conductors that prevent heat from thawing the earth below the support.

Coordinating the work force and completing the task in a little more than 3 years was a monumental feat. Over the next few years, the pipeline camps were disassembled and sold for other uses. The scarred areas have been revegetated. The caribou have been tracked to measure the effects of the pipeline's presence on their migration and calving. So far, the animals have continued to thrive, and so has Fairbanks.

A few miles northeast of Fairbanks on the Steese Highway, an above-ground portion of the trans-Alaska pipeline is visible from the road. An unimposing gravel wayside and a small, log visitors' information cabin lie on the right at Mile 8.5. Without flashing signs or fanfare, this is the most accessible point in Alaska's Interior for viewing the engineering wonder that forever changed the face of Alaska. At the viewing area, the 48-inch-diameter pipe rests on crossbars tall enough to walk under. The sign on the side of the pipeline reads "PLEASE Do not climb on the pipeline." People photograph it, ask questions of the Alyeska staff on site, and appear to be thinking, *Hmmm, so this is it?* But for those who "survived" the pipeline years in Fairbanks, the only appropriate response is "You had to be there." ■

Tips for Enjoying the Fairbanks Area

People use the terms "pre-pipeline" and "post-pipeline" to describe the years surrounding that phenomenal period in Fairbanks' history when the last big boom transformed a small town into a genuine city. Along with the escalation in home building, a handful of malls were constructed, new 4-lane highways replaced the old 2-laners, and in 1984, Fairbanksans finally experienced the pleasure of same-day national newscasts.

The airfield where the aviation pioneers landed and took off in the 1920s became the site of a new library, aptly named the Noel Wien Library, after an early-day pilot. And, during the 1980s, Fort Wainwright and Eielson Air Force Base became major players in training troops and defending North America's air space, especially considering Alaska's close proximity to the then Soviet Union.

Post-pipeline Fairbanks has been targeted by fast-food and retail giants such as Sears, Taco Bell, Sam's Club, and Fred Meyer stores. New businesses cropped up while old favorites such as J. C. Penney and Woolworth's pulled out. And when Nordstrom's clothing store decided to exit the Fairbanks market in the late 1980s, a picket line of smartly dressed women protested from the sidewalk.

Denali National Park lies 120 miles by road from Fairbanks.

On the military front, cutbacks by the federal government deeply affected Fort Wainwright when the 6th Infantry was downgraded from a division to a brigade in 1994. Still, while about 600 military personnel and their families left the state, a few hundred more people were transferred to Fairbanks with the Alyeska Pipeline Service Company.

And, although Fairbanks has long been a destination for tourists, with each new year during the 1990s, more and more visitors arrived to visit the town that gold, oil, and perseverance built.

Today, more than 300,000 people visit Fairbanks every summer, each one arriving with a notion of what he or she might expect. Most are surprised to find that Alaska is not locked in snow and ice year-round, and, in fact, its baristas can serve an espresso rivaling anything in Seattle. So, one person at a time, Fairbanks is in the business of destroying myths and presenting the realities of the Golden Heart City.

So what can you expect? How can you make the most of your Fairbanks trip? Here are some tips:

■ TRIP PLANNING, INFORMATION: Visit the Alaska Public Lands Information Center on the lower level of Courthouse Square on the corner of Third Avenue and Cushman Street. It features interpretive displays, films, lectures, and a library of Alaska books and literature. The staff is knowledgeable about the entire state and can help answer your questions or point you in the right direction. (907) 456-0527.

Also check with the Fairbanks Convention and Visitors Bureau (FCVB) for advice on where to go, what to see, and how to get there. Among other member businesses are restaurants, hotels, and bed-and-breakfasts. (907) 456-5774.

■ HISTORIC WALKING TOURS: Stop by the Visitor Information Log Cabin on First Avenue at Golden Heart Plaza for tour information and directions around town. From here you can begin a self-guided historic walking tour or join a guided group. (907) 451-1724.

The riverboat Discovery III, *a four-tiered stern-wheeler.*

■ GROUND TOURS: Many visitors have already purchased travel packages that link transportation, accommodations, and attractions through Gray Line of Alaska or Princess Tours. Independent travelers may check with the FCVB to explore tour options, including stops at Alaskaland, the Ester Gold Camp, the University of Alaska Museum, and these local favorites:

Riverboat *Discovery*. A top attraction for many years, the *Discovery* offers a cruise on the Chena and Tanana Rivers with a strong dose of local history in the narration. A stopover at a Native village setting includes an interpretation of Athabascan culture. Also, four-time Iditarod champion Susan Butcher is usually on hand to talk about sled dogs and dog mushing. (907) 479-6673.

Gold Dredge No. 8. Step into the only gold dredge in Alaska that's open to the public. Learn about how the giant soil-eating machines worked, and pan for gold. (800) 544-2206.

SUDS AND ROBERT SERVICE

SALOONS ARE AN ESSENTIAL PART of frontier lore, along with gold pokes on the bar and dancing girls on stage. Capitalizing on the region's frontier history, the valley's saloon owners offer a taste of old Alaska in décor and entertainment. Here's where to go to soak up some local flavor:

Malemute Saloon

Just west of Fairbanks off the Parks Highway in Ester, the Malemute is part of the Ester Gold Camp, which features this classic honky-

Eldorado Gold Mine. Ride the narrow-gauge railroad and discover how the miners of old extracted the gold and how it's done today with local celebrities Yukon Yonda and Dexter Clark. Gold-panning demonstrations are followed by a chance to try it yourself and keep the gold. (907) 479-7613.

■ GETTING AROUND TOWN: Rent a car at the airport (agencies provide maps) or take the city bus. The Metropolitan Area

tonk saloon with an antique bar and sawdust and peanut shells on the floor. Each summer a resident troupe performs rousing melodramas, songs, stories, and dance. Stick around for the Robert Service poetry, recited by lantern light, just as it should be. For show information or dinner reservations at the Cripple Creek Restaurant, call (907) 479-2500.

Palace Saloon

The piano playing is hot and showtime is 8:15 P.M. with the *Golden Heart Revue,* a long-running musical comedy about life in Fairbanks. This old-time saloon is among the businesses in Alaskaland's Gold Rush Town at Airport Way and Peger Road. The bar is well stocked, and the can-can cuties are high kickers. Call (907) 479-1087 for show information.

Chena Pump House

This site on the Chena River has a long and illustrious history in the gold-mining industry—and now in the food-service industry. Located at Mile 1.3 Chena Pump Road, the building was constructed by the Fairbanks Exploration Company in 1933 to pump water over the ridge and into Cripple Creek Valley. Now the building is a grand restaurant, furnished with antiques and offering an impressive menu. A solid mahogany bar is the centerpiece of the Senator's Saloon, along with its original Brunswick "Union League" pool table built in 1898 and shipped to Dawson City in 1900. For dinner reservations, call (907) 479-8452. ■

Commuter System (MACS) operates throughout the city; the main terminal is downtown on Cushman between Sixth and Seventh Avenues. (907) 459-1011.

■ AIR ACCESS: Check out the brochures at the Visitor Information Log Cabin to choose a flight to a Native village destination, book jet passage through a local travel agent, or use the phone book to find your airline of choice. Floatplane operators at the Chena Marina

Airport and Floatpond can deliver you to a remote stream or lake for excellent fly-fishing, even if you've arrived with no gear. Daily jet service is available to Barrow, Prudhoe Bay, Anchorage, Juneau, and on to Lower 48 destinations.

■ FLY/DRIVE: Contact smaller tour operators, such as Northern Alaska Tour Company at (907) 474-8600, that offer popular combination tours for folks who want to fly to Prudhoe Bay for a tour of the oil-field facilities and ride back on the remote Dalton Highway, or vice versa. Check with the FCVB at (907) 456-5774 for other options.

■ BY BUS: Independent travelers who prefer not to drive can catch the Parks Highway Express for a 2¹/₂-hour ride south to Denali National Park or on to Anchorage. (907) 479-3065.

■ BY RAIL: Arrange to ride the rails at the Alaska Railroad depot, located just behind the *Fairbanks Daily News-Miner* building off Illinois Street. Transportation to the depot from local hotels usually is available via courtesy vans or, for those on a tour, with the operator's coaches. For information on the 4-hour ride to Denali National Park or the 12-hour trip to Anchorage, call (800) 544-0552.

FOX FAVORITES

FOLLOW THE STEESE HIGHWAY north for about 10 miles to Fox and turn left. You've just entered "beautiful downtown Fox," which is really a handful of businesses, including three local favorites: the Fox Roadhouse, the Howling Dog Saloon, and the Turtle Club, each with its own unique personality. There are no polished gold-rush shows here, but you may meet some real-life gold miners who drop by to let down their hair at the roadhouse or "The Dog." Try some of the valley's best prime rib at the Turtle Club. Reservations are recommended for the Turtle Club at (907) 457-3883. ■

Snowmobiling in the White Mountains National Recreation Area.

■ PARKS, REFUGES, CONSERVATION AREAS: Launch an adventure into one of the state and federal parks that are just a short flight from Fairbanks. Contact the land management offices listed below for assistance.

U.S. Fish and Wildlife Service. The agency oversees management of the Arctic National Wildlife Refuge (ANWR), Kanuti National Wildlife Refuge, and Yukon Flats National Wildlife Refuge. Offices are in the Federal Building, 101 12th Ave. ANWR: (907) 456-0253; Kanuti: (907) 456-0329; Yukon Flats: (907) 456-0440.

National Park Service. The Fairbanks office manages Gates of the Arctic National Park and Preserve, and Yukon–Charley Rivers National Park and Preserve. (907) 456-0281.

Bureau of Land Management. The BLM manages a number of public campgrounds and waysides, including sites along the Dalton Highway, formerly the pipeline Haul Road. It also offers

text continues on page 88

GOING FOR THE GOLD

GOLD DOES SOMETHING TO PEOPLE. It makes converts with the first touch. In the jewelry stores, gift shops, and assayer's office, it's all the same. Smiling, the man or woman hefts the gold up and down, enjoying the muted glitter, the knobby, dimpled dead weight of a nugget in the palm of the hand. Then the inevitable question: *How much is this worth?*

In the Tanana Valley, they can tell you that, as well as how to distinguish the difference between fool's gold and real gold, where to look for gold, and how to pan it. At any number of local jewelers, you can choose a nugget that came from an Interior stream and have it custom-made into a piece of jewelry. And for out-of-towners, as well as for the locals who get to show them around, it's always a treat to stop by either or both of two popular attractions that capitalize on Fairbanks' mining history: Gold Dredge No. 8 and the Eldorado Gold Mine.

Gold Dredge No. 8 is an old lady that's been gussied up for visitors. This grand old dredge shoveled many thousands of tons of dirt, rocks, and gold since it was built in 1928 until its retirement in 1959. Operated by Gray Line of Alaska and located off the Steese Highway at Goldstream Road, the dredge is a fine example of the floating gold-processing ships that were most prevalent during the 1930s and '40s. Visitors can explore the interior and learn how this massive piece of equipment worked. Gold-panning demonstrations are followed by opportunities to try it for yourself. A gift shop and museum are located on the premises, and lunch is available.

Farther up the Steese Highway, just past Fox at Mile 1.2 Elliott Highway, is the Eldorado Gold Mine, where visitors board a narrow-gauge railroad train for a trip back through time. As the train slows near a cabin, a sourdough demonstrates how his old rocker-box works. Next the train enters a broad tunnel that holds fossilized bones and tusks, and a miner explains how placer gold is deposited and mined. Finally, it pulls into an old-time frontier town, and everybody disembarks to watch a modern-day mining couple run a load of pay dirt through the sluice box using a backhoe. The next step is panning for yourself, and you get to keep the gold you find. You can have your gold weighed and made into a piece of jewelry on the spot. The gift shop offers clothing, books, knickknacks, gold-nugget jewelry, and free cookies and coffee.

Or, for a true taste of Fairbanks' mining history, drive the Steese Highway north to just past milepost 16. There you'll find the monument to Felix Pedro near the creek that made him famous and launched the rush that established Fairbanks. ■

Dexter Clark greets visitors to the Eldorado Gold Mine.

ICE ART CHAMPIONSHIPS

FAIRBANKS IS COLD, and it has plenty of ice—so what better way to exploit its natural resources than to host an annual event for ice carvers? Each March, top ice carvers from all over the world converge for the World Ice Art Championships. The Fairbanks ice they carve has come to be known as the "arctic diamond." The thick blocks of ice taken from a local gravel pit are exquisite: clear, shimmering, and nearly bubble-free. To the competitors, the ice is near perfection, the best in the world.

Alongside the Chena River, visitors pay a fee to meander through the ice art park, photograph the entries, and watch the carvers at work. Set among the spruce in the sometimes below-zero temperatures of mid-March, the intricately carved entries are lit with brilliantly colored lights. Sometimes the carvers create entire tableaus in ice: merry-go-rounds, log cabins and miners, and whimsical figures locked in gravity- and heat-defying loops.

The annual ice art competition overlaps with the events of the week-long Fairbanks Winter Carnival. Activities include a parka parade, camp stove chili cook-off, snowshoe softball, and more. For information on either event, call (907) 452-1105. ■

printed materials on ways to enjoy local conservation areas. The Northern Field Office is located at 1150 University Ave. (907) 474-2302.

Alaska Division of Parks and Outdoor Recreation. The Northern Area Office of the state's parks system manages many thousands of acres of public parks and recreation sites. The office is located at 3700 Airport Way. (907) 451-2695. Questions about Department of Natural Resources Division of Forestry or DNR's

Flyfishing on the Chena River.

Division of Land may be answered in the same office building. (907) 451-2700.

Alaska Department of Fish and Game. All questions on licensing for hunters, fishers, and trappers should be directed to the Fairbanks Regional Office, located in the restored farmhouse at Creamer's Field Migratory Waterfowl Refuge, 1300 College Road. (907) 459-7200. For sportfishing information, call 459-7385; for hunting information, call 459-7306; for wildlife conservation information, call 459-7213.

■ NATIVE VILLAGES: Several Athabascan villages are just a short hop away and welcome visitors. Visit Bettles, Fort Yukon, a Stevens Village fish camp on the Tanana River, or fly north to the Eskimo communities of Barrow, Kotzebue, Nome, or Anaktuvuk Pass to learn more about Alaska's first people. The FCVB has more information at (907) 456-5774.

■ GOLF: Play at the North Star Golf Club. While it's no Augusta, the club offers a special visitor rate for playing its nine holes; (907) 457-GOLF. The Fairbanks Golf and Country Club, off Farmers

Loop Road, offers more of the same. Hazards include an occasional moose crossing the green. (907) 479-6555.

■ ROADSIDE WILDERNESS: Visit one of the popular local wilderness areas, such as the Chena River State Recreation Area, which stretches from mileposts 26 to 53 along Chena Hot Springs Road. It's easily accessible for day-trippers, picnickers, and explorers who can follow 35 miles of marked trail or climb the Granite Tors outcropping.

Southeast of Fairbanks near Mile 17 Richardson Highway, the Chena Lakes Recreation Area offers camping, swimming, boating, fishing, and picnicking within a short drive. Drive another 25 miles to reach the turnoff for Harding Lake State Recreation Area.

The Fairbanks North Star Borough manages Chena Lakes; call (907) 488-1655 for details. The other two wilderness areas are managed by the Alaska Division of Parks and Outdoor Recreation; call (907) 451-2695 for more information.

■ SKIING: Cross-country and downhill enthusiasts will find trails and slopes to their liking. For cross-country skiing or skijoring, visit Birch Hill Recreation Area on the northeast edge of town off the Steese Highway. Downhill skiers can choose among Cleary Summit or Skiland, both near Mile 20 Steese Highway, or Moose Mountain Ski Resort on Spinach Creek Road on Murphy Dome. Check the phone book for local listings or contact the FCVB at (907) 456-5774 for more information.

■ THE ARTS: Attend the Fairbanks Summer Arts Festival, hosted by the city on the UAF campus in early August. Students study under guest jazz-to-classics musicians, and the community enjoys a week of evening performances. (907) 474-8869.

The Festival of Native Arts in late February attracts Native dancers, singers, and craftspeople from all over the country. The public is invited to dance performances and craft fairs at the University of Alaska. (907) 474-7181.

Summer-long performances by the Shakespeare Theatre troupe are held in an outdoor theater at Birch Hill Recreation Area,

Shopping at Farmers' Market on a perfect summer day.

off the Steese Highway. Check with the FCVB at (907) 456-5774 for dates, prices, and performance times on these and any other current arts attractions.

Summer visitors can observe Alaska Native games and dances, and learn all about the area's first people in performances titled *Northern Inua*, held at the University of Alaska Museum's Aurora Dome. (907) 474-7505. ◼

Recommended Reading

Alaska Geographic Society. *Alaska's Great Interior*, Vol. 7, No. 1, 1980.

Chandonnet, Fern, ed. *Alaska at War, 1941–1945: The Forgotten War Remembered*. Anchorage: Alaska at War Committee, 1995.

Cloe, John Haile. *Top Cover for America*. Anchorage: Anchorage Chapter, Air Force Association and Pictorial Histories Publishing Co., 1984.

Cole, Dermot. *Amazing Pipeline Stories*. Seattle: Epicenter Press, 1997.

Cole, Terrence, ed. *The Alaska Journal®*, Vol. 15, No. 2. "An Expedition to the Copper, Tanana and Koyukuk Rivers in 1885" by Lieutenant Henry T. Allen. Anchorage: Alaska Northwest Publishing Co., 1985.

Cole, Terrence. *The Cornerstone on College Hill*. Fairbanks: University of Alaska Press, 1994.

_____. *Crooked Past: The History of a Frontier Mining Camp*. Fairbanks: University of Alaska Press, 1991.

_____. *Ghosts of the Gold Rush: A Walking Tour of Fairbanks*. Revised and edited by Jane G. Haigh and Jon Nielson. Fairbanks: Tanana-Yukon Historical Society, 1987.

Hunt, William R. *North of 53°*. New York: Macmillan Publishing Co., 1974.

Huntington, Sidney, as told to Jim Rearden. *Shadows on the Koyukuk: An Alaskan Native's Life Along the River*. Seattle: Alaska Northwest Books, 1993.

Mitchell, Donald Craig. *Sold American: The Story of Alaska Natives and Their Land, 1867–1959*. Hanover, New Hampshire: University Press of New England, 1997.

Morgan, Lael. *Alaska's Native People*. Vol. 16, No. 3. Anchorage: Alaska Geographic Society, 1979.

_____. *Good Time Girls of the Alaska-Yukon Gold Rush*. Seattle: Epicenter Press, 1998.

Murie, Margaret E. *Two in The Far North*. Seattle: Alaska Northwest Books, 1997.

Naske, Claus-M., and L. J. Rowinski. *Fairbanks: A Pictorial History*. Norfolk, VA: The Donning Co., 1981.

Ritter, Harry. *Alaska's History*. Seattle: Alaska Northwest Books, 1993.

Wickersham, James. *Old Yukon*. St. Paul: West Publishing Co., 1938.

Wold, Jo Anne. *Fairbanks: The $200 Million Gold Rush Town*. Fairbanks: Wold Press, 1971.

_____. *This Old House*. Anchorage: Alaska Northwest Publishing Co., 1976.

INDEX

*Page numbers in **bold face** indicate photographs.*

Alaska Northwest Books is proud to publish another book in its Alaska Pocket Guide series, designed with the curious traveler in mind. Ask for more books in this series at your favorite bookstore, or contact Alaska Northwest Books.™

ALASKA NORTHWEST BOOKS™

An imprint of Graphic Arts Center Publishing Company
P.O. Box 10306, Portland, OR 97296-0306
503-226-2402; www.gacpc.com